Mae Franking's
My Chinese Marriage

Tiam and Mae Franking with Nelson, circa 1913.

KATHERINE ANNE PORTER

Mae Franking's
My Chinese Marriage
An Annotated Edition

Edited by Holly Franking
Foreword by Joan Givner

UNIVERSITY OF TEXAS PRESS
AUSTIN

First edition, 1991

Requests for permission to reproduce material from this
work should be sent to Permissions, University of Texas
Press, Box 7819, Austin, TX 78713-7819.

∞ The paper used in this publication meets the
minimum requirements of American National Standard for
Information Sciences—Permanence of Paper for Printed
Library Materials, ANSI Z39.48-1984.

Library of Congress Cataloging-in-Publication Data

Franking, Mae M.
  Mae Franking's "My Chinese marriage" : an annotated
edition / Katherine Anne Porter ; edited by Holly Franking ;
foreword by Joan Givner. — 1st ed.
      p.   cm.
  Includes bibliographical references.
  ISBN 0-292-75132-X (alk. paper)
  1. Franking, Mae M.   2. Married women—China—
Biography.   3. Americans—China—Biography.
4. China—Social life and customs—1912–1949.
I. Porter, Katherine Anne, 1890–1980.
II. Franking, Holly.   III. Title.
CT1828.F73A3   1991
951.04′092—dc20
[B]   91-12698
                                                  CIP

*This book is dedicated
to my parents,
Elizabeth O'Connor Franking
and
Nelson W. Franking.*

CONTENTS

FOREWORD
by Joan Givner

We can only speculate on the reactions of Katherine Anne Porter and Mae Watkins Franking to each other during the two weeks they spent together seventy years ago. They were both strong, talented women, born in the same year, one destined for literary fame and a very long life and the other already infected with the tuberculosis which would shortly cause her death.

I imagine that Mae was impressed by her counterpart's aristocratic bearing and beauty—the celebrated charm. Porter, for her part, would be conscious of Mae's superior education, her travels to distant places, and her status as widow and mother of three. She would also, I suspect, be a little unnerved by the realization that Mae's husband had died of the disease with which Porter herself had recently fought a hard battle. Hearing Mae's stories of the ostracism that resulted from her interracial marriage, seeing her strained by grief, robbed by death of her beloved Tiam, Porter would understand the stigma of pariahdom, the sense of loss, and alienation. I imagine she was warmly sympathetic, but, on the other hand, she might have recoiled from such visible reminders of her own griefs.

Over the years, Porter made several remarks, generally dismissive, about her work on Mae's story. She said that the task was a dreary one, that she toiled over it wearily for several months and took it with her to Mexico in late 1920.[1] Sometimes the references were oblique, as in these paragraphs at the beginning of "St. Augustine and the Bullfight":

Adventure. The word has become a little stale to me, because it has been applied too often to the dull physical exploits of professional "adventurers" who write books about it, if they know how to write; if not, they hire ghosts who quite often can't write either.

. . . .

W. B. Yeats remarked—I cannot find the passage now, so must say it in other words—that the unhappy man (unfortunate?) was one whose ad-

ventures outran his capacity for experience, capacity for experience being,
I should say, roughly equal to the faculty of understanding what has happened to one.[2]

When Edward Schwartz was compiling his 1953 bibliography, Porter wrote
him that *My Chinese Marriage* "is a mere setting down of someone else's story,
nothing of my own." Of a collection of articles on marriage to which she had
written an introduction she wrote: "This book and *My Chinese Marriage*
should have no place in the list of my works."[3]

Finally she wrote the book's epitaph when she inscribed a copy at the University of Maryland's Katherine Anne Porter Room. She said that she took dic-
tation from Mae's words and that they both acted with integrity and inno-
cence, but the result was false because Mae was unable to understand what
had happened to her.[4] Again Porter evoked the words from Yeats which had
impressed her, although she never could recall where they came from.[5]

We might attribute the belittling remarks to Porter's unwillingness to coun-
tenance an untidy start to her career. She preferred to erase the years of ap-
prenticeship in journalism and superimpose the magical experience of being
"tossed into print" by an editor "with such an air of it being all in the day's
work, which it was, I went away in a dazzle of joy, not in the least thinking of
myself as 'discovered'—I had known where I was all along—nor looking forward to the future as a 'career.'"[6]

There is, however, in Porter's repudiation of her ghostwriting assignment,
something else at stake. In order to understand it, one must recognize how
much of Porter herself is contained (her words to Schwartz notwithstanding)
in the book. When certain passages from *My Chinese Marriage* are placed beside others from, say, *Ship of Fools,* it is evident that, in spite of a forty-year
time gap, the same hand, eye, ear, and general sensibility inform both works.
Take, for instance, these descriptions of ships coming into harbor:

> Yet from every ship the flags were flying and dipping in courtesy to the
> harbor and all in it, the little bands on every deck were playing their hop-
> pity tunes, the crews and the officers were at their stations, all paint-fresh,
> fit and ready, in good discipline.
>
> *Ship of Fools,* 495

> . . . our bouncing little ship . . . stood to, out from port, and sampans
> came to meet us. Like giant fish bobbing and dipping and swaying upon

the waves, these sampans with their great eyes painted on each side of the prow and their curious, up-curved sterns, came towards us in a gala-fleet, rowed by lean, over-muscled men in faded blue cotton garments.

My Chinese Marriage, 102

Porter was always stimulated by the sight from a passing ship of an island with its distinct terrain, flowers, and foliage. She described in excited letters to friends her first glimpse of Bermuda in the spring of 1929.[7] She described both in letters and in her novel the pleasure of seeing and smelling the Isle of Wight from the deck of the *Vera* in 1931. The following paragraphs are Jenny Brown's view of Tenerife from the *Vera* and Margaret's (pseudonym for Mae) first sight of her husband's home province in southern China:

In the morning, the engine gave three loud thumps, and stopped. Jenny put her head out, and there at her very porthole was Santa Cruz de Tenerife, a jagged long rock indeed, sown with palms, smothered in bougainvillea, the flat square houses perched and huddled on cliff-steep levels hacked out as with chisels.

Ship of Fools, 364

As we were being rowed in to the mainland, we were near enough to the island to see quite plainly the tile-roofed houses surrounded by arched verandas, repeated again and again in long, undulating lines that gave a pleasantly lacy effect. . . . Jagged cacti shot up among the bulbous rocks and everywhere the scarlet poinsettia set the hills aglow with patches of brilliant color.

. . . .

With enormous curiosity, I peeped through the curtain-flaps, which were transparent from within. We were passing through the town that lay along the water's edge—a bright, open little place, where the small houses, with curved tiled roofs, hugged the ground.

My Chinese Marriage, 103–104

Akin to Porter's delight in seeing a ship come into harbor is her feeling for the traveler returning home after a long absence, an experience she expressed in her poem "Anniversary in a Country Cemetery."[8] Often the feeling of homecoming turns out to be illusory, for the wanderer is, essentially, a "homeless one":

A short young fellow . . . rushed uncontrollably up the stairs to the rail of the upper deck and poised there on his spread toes, his gaze soaring out from him like a bird to the little towns lying at the foot and climbing up the sides of the stony island. Oblivious, smiling, the round instinctive eyes filled with tears. Even as Wilhelm Freytag saw him and envied him his homecoming, even as Jenny said, "It must be wonderful to cry for joy!"

Ship of Fools, 365

Emotion surged up in me. I wished to cry for joy in this home-coming, for it was our real home-coming together, and I felt a secret share in all the life my husband had known here.

My Chinese Marriage, 105

The above is not an exhaustive list of comparisons, for students of Porter must not be deprived of the satisfaction of finding their own parallels. But one particular passage demands attention because its counterpart is a work by Porter which is not readily available.

A climactic passage of *My Chinese Marriage* is the lyrical description of Margaret and Chan-King (pseudonym for Tiam) sitting together in the garden on the eve of their departure from his ancestral home. The mood is elegiac as they speak with foreboding of love, immortality, and eternity. Because of their position in the garden, their vows to each other take place against a backdrop of sounds and impressions which evoke the whole teeming life of the family enclave:

From Mother's apartments came the sound of her young nephew's voice as he chanted his morrow's lessons. We heard the subdued merriment of two little maids, teasing each other in the hall beyond. Along the outer path a sedan-chair passed with rhythmic sway, the bamboo supports creaking a soft accompaniment to the pad-pad of the bearer's sandaled feet.

From varying distances came the clang of a brass gong, shuddering on the stillness, the staccato sound of slender bamboo sticks shaken together in a cylindrical box, the measured beat of a small drum-rattle, as the different street vendors announced their wares. Over the hills, now purple in the twilight, the round moon swung leisurely into the violet sky. Strange breaths of incense wafted about us. The sea-breeze stirred the branches of a nearby dragon's-eye tree, where the ripening fruit-balls tapped gently against each other like little swaying lanterns.

My Chinese Marriage, 167

Porter's readers will recall that a similar vantage point is chosen by the grandmother and Aunt Nannie Gay of *The Old Order* as they sit sewing and reminiscing together. Their choice of location is part of their "domestic strategy" and allows them to keep watch (more or less) on the doings of the children and servants.[9]

The passage also resembles very closely an extended description of Porter's living quarters when she worked on *My Chinese Marriage.* "In a Mexican Patio" is a fifteen-page essay which Porter submitted to the *Oil Journal* in Fort Worth soon after she was forced to leave Mexico in the summer of 1921.[10] The first-person narrator describes the sounds which filter up to her window and convey a sense of the busy, varied life of the place: the sound of a child singing, the splash of a fountain playing, and the slap of hands making tortillas. In this extended meditation, the narrator thinks sadly of death at dusk, but in the morning she has a sense of immortality.

These comparisons show similar details, perceived from the same point of view and described in the same turns of phrase. Of greater importance, however, are the thematic links between *My Chinese Marriage* and some of Porter's most successful fictions.

Closest in time is "Holiday," a story published in the early 1960s but virtually finished in 1924.[11] Although the story was based on a visit Porter made to a farm on the Texas-Louisiana border, it is informed chiefly by the experience of her first marriage into a rich Texas ranching and land-owning family of Swiss-German descent. The Müllers are isolated by their German speech and culture and by the self-sufficiency of the productive farm. In the midst of this self-contained family, the narrator is in turn isolated. She cannot speak their language but takes pleasure in her remoteness from their daily concerns. She occupies an attic room, writes letters, and listens to the sounds of the swirling life of the house. When she joins the family for dinner, her anomalous state is accentuated by her position on the men's side of the table.

The narrator's situation in the patriarchal Müller family is very similar to that of Margaret when she is left by Chan-King at his family's self-contained ancestral estate in southern China. She cannot speak the language, becomes adept at communicating through gestures, and spends a great deal of time writing letters. "Those children write long letters to each other, fifteen and twenty pages at a time," marvels her Chinese mother-in-law. Margaret contemplates the vestiges of the patriarchal culture—the bound feet and long curled fingernails which restrict the activity of the women and, in the countryside, the sinister widows' arches, stone memorials to the suicide of newly widowed women. Although the barbaric custom of allowing widows to immolate themselves is forbidden, the sense that a woman without a husband has no status and no function remains. On the whole, Margaret is uneasy in her appointed ceremonial role as first daughter-in-law, and she and her husband decide to leave China and return to the United States. However, after he has died and Margaret, at the end of her story, is alone, she experiences her widowhood as a ghostlike state in which she has no life, only memories of the past. The final paragraph of *My Chinese Marriage* shows a narrator torn between the roles of independent woman and one whose worth depends upon her relationship with a man. The narrator of "Holiday" shows a similar ambivalence.

Because of these tensions experienced by her younger self, the character of an enduring elderly woman was appealing to Porter, and she created memorable portraits of grandmothers—Ellen Weatherall and Sophia Jane Rhea. In "The Old Order," Miranda grows up in an ancestral home presided over by the grandmother who is assisted by her lifelong black companion, Nannie Gay. The description of the husband's ancestral home in *My Chinese Marriage* is quite similar to Miranda's. Both are sprawling homes, staffed by many servants in hot southern provinces. The ruling patriarch is absent on honorable business as are most of his sons. Accordingly, like an empress, the elderly mother presides as his surrogate over the household. She too is assisted and supported by her lifelong companion.

That Porter based her grandmother characters on her own strong grandmother, Catherine Anne Skaggs Porter, is a well-known fact. Porter grew up in a home presided over by a woman, with her father relegated to the subservient role of an elder child. Consequently, Porter's fictions have often depicted strong, resourceful women compared with whom the male characters seem feeble and ineffective. Such a situation is a feature of *My Chinese Marriage*. At Margaret's own home in Ann Arbor, her father is barely mentioned, while her mother provides comfort and advice to the lovers. The portrait of the mother-in-law is the most fully drawn in the book, and the relationship between Margaret and her mother-in-law is depicted with as much (if not greater) intensity as that between Margaret and Chan-King.

Another story with strong thematic links to *My Chinese Marriage* is "Pale Horse, Pale Rider." The story's basis in Porter's experience as a journalist on the *Rocky Mountain News* in Denver has again been well documented. There is such a close connection between that story and the articles Porter wrote in 1918–1919 that the existence of a lost version written near to the time seems very likely. At the end of "Pale Horse, Pale Rider," Miranda has contracted a deadly disease, has almost died, and has survived only to discover that her lover has died from the same contagion. She emerges from the hospital feeling like a resuscitated corpse returning to the world—but dangerously drawn to the past and to the dead. Similarly, Margaret, after the death of Chan-King, declares her history finished and is drawn back to memories of her husband and her lost life in China.

Tuberculosis is barely mentioned in either story, and yet the specter of that disease lies over both works as it did over the lives of Porter and Mae Franking. Porter, in 1918, had just survived a two-year battle against it, and I believe that the shadow of death that pervades "Pale Horse, Pale Rider" is that of the white plague, as tuberculosis was called. Mae's husband suffered from TB and finally died of it in 1919. Mae herself was to die of the disease seven years later.

Feminist critics have shown how often the links between women writers have been erased. In discussions of Mary Shelley's *Frankenstein,* for example, Percy Bysshe Shelley used to be mentioned more often than Mary Wollstonecraft. Sometimes women writers themselves, conscious of their lack of formal education, felt the need to establish their credentials by mentioning writers of a stature and complexity that I suspect made them too intimidating to serve as useful models. As Virginia Woolf said:

> It is useless to go to the great men writers for help, however much one
> may go to them for pleasure. Lamb, Browne, Thackeray, Newman, Sterne,
> Dickens, De Quincey . . . never helped a woman yet, though she may
> have learnt a few tricks of them and adapted them to her use. The weight,
> pace, stride of a man's mind are too unlike her for her to lift anything
> substantial from his successfully. The ape is too distant to be sedulous.[12]

When Katherine Anne Porter spoke of early influences, she evoked writers of impressive stature. She told a credulous Eudora Welty that she had discovered Joyce for herself, having found a copy of *Ulysses* in a second-hand bookstore in Galveston.[13] As she told an interviewer:

> That was the turning point of my life, when I read the Shakespeare sonnets,
> and then all at one blow, all of Dante. . . . Oh, and I read of all kinds of
> poetry—Homer, Ronsard, all the old French poets in translation. We also
> had a very good library of—well, you might say secular philosophers.[14]

As with many of Porter's statements, these words are not entirely true and not entirely false. It is possible to find echoes of Shakespeare's sonnets, for instance, in her short stories. But I think she was also influenced by what she read in the popular magazines of her day. I suspect that Ring Lardner's "Hair-cut" influenced "Magic" and that Mazo de la Roche's Adeline Whiteoak influenced Porter's grandmother characters. Yet she suppressed her debt to popular writers, as she did for similar reasons her debt to Mae Watkins Franking.

We shall never know conclusively (unless Mae's formless manuscript should surface unexpectedly) the extent to which Porter's treatment shaped Mae's story. But I think it is safe to assume that Porter's prolonged struggle with the task was a crucial part of her development as a writer. It forms the transition between her work as a journalist and her work as a fiction writer.

Katherine Anne Porter and Mae Watkins Franking were in some ways a complementary pair. Mae had lived through experiences which provided the substance of a successful book. But although her copious letters show that she had writing ability, she was unable to complete the task herself. Perhaps she was too ill and dispirited, perhaps too occupied with caring for her three children. In any event, the manuscript was forwarded to Porter, an experienced journalist, used to turning out copy on demand, but still unsure about the usefulness of her own experiences in providing the proper stuff of fiction.

Porter went to Mexico and found enough experience there for such fiction. She used that experience in some stories, but she learned eventually that it was her own country, her own speech, and her own past life which would yield her the greatest benefits. Yet her work on *My Chinese Marriage* predated that crucial piece of knowledge, and in rejecting that project she was rejecting her younger naïve self. It is a common human trait, after all, to be hardest on those people and things that mirror what embarrasses us most in ourselves.

My Chinese Marriage, then, is important to Porter studies because it illuminates a gap in Porter's creative development and opens up a new area deserving of study by scholars. And apart from the contribution it makes to the record of an important American writer, it must not be overlooked that the history of Mae and Tiam has its own value as a profoundly moving story. It stands squarely on its own feet, so its republication is an additional cause for celebration.

Finally, I must add a personal note. The biographer is often assisted by the kindness of those who share memories and materials which illuminate the life-in-progress, giving time and handing over information that surfaces in family attics and archives. I see from my file of letters that my relationship with the grandchildren of Mae Watkins Franking dates back to the later 1970s. It has been one of the joys of my project, an association characterized by civility and generosity and blossoming into a warm friendship, and now culminating in this book.

ACKNOWLEDGMENTS

I wish to thank several people for their help in bringing this book about: my mother, Elizabeth Franking, for suggesting that I might do something about the wonderful story my grandmother left; my aunt, Cecile Franking Wu, who kept the letters of her parents safe and secure "lo these many years," for graciously passing them on to me; Joan Givner for her valuable insights; the staff of the University of Texas Press for making the process of this publication a pleasant one, especially Frankie Westbrook, humanities editor, for her generous help and sure guidance. And, finally, I'd like to offer a special thanks to my husband, John Slegman, for his able criticism and loving encouragement.

H.F.

INTRODUCTION

by Holly Franking

Before "Pale Horse, Pale Rider," "Flowering Judas," and "Hacienda," before "The Leaning Tower," "Noon Wine," and *Ship of Fools,* there was *My Chinese Marriage.*[1] In 1920 Gertrude Emerson, an associate editor of *Asia: The American Magazine on the Orient,* hired Katherine Anne Porter to rewrite the autobiography of the marriage of Mae Watkins and Tiam Hock Franking.[2] After visiting Mae Franking at her home in Ann Arbor, Michigan,[3] Porter took the manuscript back to New York with her, then to Mexico, where she spent several months working on it.[4]

Asia published *My Chinese Marriage* in serial form in its June, July, August, and September issues of 1921. Mae Franking's story of an interracial marriage between a Scotch-Irish woman and a Chinese man stirred some controversy. *Asia* editor John Foord denied that the story encouraged interracial marriage. Instead, he stated that "it is making a real contribution to the wealth of human experience."[5] In spite of the controversy, Duffield and Company subsequently published the articles in book form, and the book went through several printings.

As for the authorship, from 1921 to 1952, the cards in the Library of Congress listed M. T. F. and/or Mae Franking as the author of *My Chinese Marriage.* Cross-references to Katherine Anne Porter did not appear until 1953. These cards also quote Porter as saying this book "is a mere setting down of someone else's story, nothing of my own."[6]

Nevertheless, scholars have been known to go against the expressed wishes of authors before, and this case offers compelling reasons for them to do so again. For instance, when Porter told the compiler of the Schwartz bibliography about *My Chinese Marriage,* she apparently did not request that it be excluded along with the other hired work, *What Price Marriage.*[7] Furthermore, a few years before the cross-references were made between Porter and Franking in the card catalog, Porter worked as a consultant at the Library of Congress. Yet she apparently did not take steps to delete or change these references. Such incidents suggest that Porter may not have been as interested in keeping *My Chinese Marriage* off her list of works as she seems to have thought she was. So, although Porter said *My Chinese Marriage* "should have no place in the list of my works," the fact remains that all her bibliographies do list it.[8] Consequently, the question of whether or not to include it is a moot one.[9]

Unfortunately, no extant copy of Mae Franking's original manuscript has been found. Such a finding would establish precisely what changes Porter made to it. Perhaps the manuscript will yet turn up either in the holdings of *Asia* or among the papers of Gertrude Emerson or someone else connected with the magazine, such as Lowell Thomas, who was also an associate editor.

Nevertheless, it might be supposed that Porter did not want *My Chinese Marriage* included on her list simply because the content was not hers. Even so, Porter's setting down of this story does make the style Porter's rather than Mae Franking's, unlike *What Price Marriage,* which is a collection of essays by well-known authors.[10]

Of more importance is the fact that *My Chinese Marriage* was written at the beginning of Porter's writing career and that it contains over twenty-three thousand words, making it her longest work except for *Ship of Fools.* As a result, this work offers literary scholars a unique opportunity to study Porter's development as an artist. Joan Givner makes this same point in her Porter biography when she says that Porter was influenced more by her work on *My Chinese Marriage* than she would have willingly admitted.[11]

Thus, the purpose of this annotated version of *My Chinese Marriage* is not to ask whether or not to include this book in Porter's oeuvre, but rather to ask, "What is the rightful place of *My Chinese Marriage* among the collected works of Katherine Anne Porter?"

To help readers answer this question, I have provided a summary of the most important events in the courtship and marriage of Mae and Tiam Franking. The source for this summary is a personal collection of over five hundred letters, newspaper articles, photographs, and other documents written by or about Mae and Tiam.[12] This summary also contains notations that point out differences between it and the published version of *My Chinese Marriage.* By comparing these two accounts and the writing styles of Porter and Mae Franking, the reader can see how Porter's version differed from the actual story and, more important, how Porter imprinted her own inimitable style upon it.[13]

Summary of the Courtship and Marriage
of Mae and Tiam Franking

Mae Munro Watkins of Ann Arbor, Michigan, first met Tiam Hock Franking, of Amoy, China, when they both attended Ann Arbor High School.[14] Mae was seventeen; Tiam, nineteen. The year was 1907. Each planned to attend the University of Michigan upon graduation.[15] Mae wanted to teach German and Latin; Tiam wanted to obtain a law degree, specializing in international law. Such a degree would be useful when he returned to China to work in his father's export business.[16]

Within a couple of years, the infatuation between Mae and Tiam intensified. Because they were so young, Mr. and Mrs. Watkins suggested that the two separate for a year to make sure of their feelings for each other. Tiam agreed and enrolled in Grand Rapids High School.[17] The night before he left, Mae wrote a letter to herself which she was to reread one year later on 29 August 1910. It ended with the question: "A year from now how will this present moment appear to us . . . as a sweet memory or a 'low of promise' for the future? Oh, well, a year from now and I shall answer easily—it will not matter then. But, ah, the interval between!" She pressed one tiny violet into the pages and sealed the envelope.

As for that interval between, from August through December and well into the new year of 1910, the letters flowed from 219 South Ingalls Street, Ann Arbor, to 195 Lyon, Grand Rapids, and back. At first they arrived with hesitant salutations: "Dear Miss Watkins" or "Dear Friend Tiam" and closed formally with "I remain as ever." But the pages themselves were crammed with descriptions of their teachers and new classmates, of their courses and class schedules, of their examinations and term paper topics, of their poetry and oration contests both won and lost. More important, they showed a deepening sense of sympathy, understanding, and love growing between them. Tiam finally expressed joy that Mae loved him. At first Mae denied that her simple words were betraying unconscious feelings. But then she happily conceded that he was right. She closed with a simple affirmation: "Tiam, I love you" (22 April 1910).

In the spring of 1910, Tiam graduated from Grand Rapids High School. He returned to Ann Arbor and roomed at 917 East Huron Street. Shortly afterward Tiam declared to Mae, "Beyond any rational doubt, dearest, you have drawn my whole heart."[18] Unfortunately, Mae's friends and relatives, which included a medley of Watkinses and Munros, began to express concern about Mae's relationship with the Chinese youth. Interracial marriages at that time were discouraged by a host of legal and social restrictions (27 July 1910). Nevertheless, Mae took a stand for herself and stated in a letter to one aunt that in spite of what the others said, she did know her duty to her parents, her country, her flag, and even to her future children. And besides, she saw another duty, that to herself and to Tiam (26 October 1910).

Tiam began his studies at the University of Michigan Law School in the fall of 1910. While at Michigan, Tiam received letters from his parents, urging him to break off his relationship with the American girl. He, too, was reminded of his duty to his family, to his country, and to his intended bride. As was the custom, at a very early age Tiam's parents had betrothed him to the young daughter of a friend. Since Tiam was the eldest son, his future wife would one day replace his mother as head of the ancestral home. Therefore, Tiam's choice of a bride would affect his entire family. Tiam respectfully replied, hoping to explain his love for Mae, which to his parents signified defiance. Gradually, the letters from brothers, friends, in-laws, clergy, and, finally, his parents stopped. Irrevocably, Tiam was cut off from both his past and the future he had planned.

Mae's parents did not want a breach with their daughter. Also, they did not feel the same cultural bias as the others. Still, they were concerned that the prejudice against interracial marriage, on both sides of the Pacific, would make life hard for the couple. Mae's sister, Gwen, who was ten years younger than Mae, bore the brunt of the prejudice. As a grade school student, she had to endure the jibes of classmates and adults who lacked the courage to say what they thought directly to Mae and Tiam or to Mr. and Mrs. Watkins.

Gradually, Mae and Tiam became estranged from their own cultures. They accepted their situation regretfully, yet, because of their love, willingly. Consequently, they became everything to each other—parents, friends, advisers. The first real cultural crisis in their relationship came when Tiam thought that they also should become lovers in the fullest sense.[19] Tiam clung "to his belief that a girl would want a man, if she loved him at all" (5 July 1911). Mae, on the other hand, tried to explain her principle: "That a true woman, no matter how deeply she loves a man, until the time when she's bound to him by the sacred ties of marriage will consider her most sacred self first . . . the self which she hopes to give into the keeping of her husband alone" (6 July 1911).

When Tiam's pressure on Mae increased,[20] she seemed to withdraw from him. This caused Tiam to doubt her love: "It has been hard, harder, than you can ever know, my darling, to love as I have loved—but if I failed to be able to make you love me . . . when [the] whole world seems sad without having things right between us" then perhaps we should end everything here (15 June 1911). He wrote this comment as he prepared to leave for Fort Wayne, Indiana, on business. In the letters that followed, Mae tried to make him understand: "I have not changed, dear Tiam, my love is the same. . . . But to be separated from you, when I love you, by the cold wall of your theory. . . . Oh, Tiam, where now is all the endearing tenderness that I knew and loved in you?" (8 August 1911). In another letter she added, "I have been thinking about what you said about the flame of love dying without a supply of oil. But it doesn't always die out . . . sometimes it burns into the heart and soul" (May 1911). Mae's apparent lecture on true love offended Tiam, who felt that she had misunderstood his motives if she suspected that "he could easily and freely give anything so important without regard to honor and respect . . . for to give so without love is a shame." Nevertheless, he conceded to her: "I love you and I want you too—but when you can't feel natural & content with me, I must abide by your wish and what your heart dictates" (11 July 1911). With this important reconciliation seemingly behind them, Mae was elated, and Tiam could write with joy to her from Springfield, Ohio: "Love makes all things new, alive, & significant . . . love is success, love is happiness, love is life" (26 August 1911).

Mae enrolled in the Department of Literature, Science, and the Arts of the University of Michigan in August 1911 to study Latin and German. She and Tiam were together again and happy about their studies. It was not long before they decided to marry after graduation. They shared their decision first with Mae's parents. Mr. and Mrs. Watkins acquiesced, concealing their concerns. Tiam's father's response was a brief if polite refusal. Tiam was disappointed at not receiving his father's blessing. He also understood that he must now support himself and, shortly, a wife.

By spring of 1912, Tiam had done well, keeping up with his law studies, maintaining an active social life with other Chinese students, working part time by teaching at the YMCA, and selling subscriptions for the *Review of Reviews*. But as more people became aware of their plans for marriage, Mae and Tiam felt increasingly isolated, except for Mae's immediate family and some of their closest college friends. Yet it was not an unhappy time for them, secure as they were in their love and life-plan. Still, the combined pressures of studies, finances, and family opposition took its toll on them. After a year or more of agonizing soul-searching, Mae finally gave in to Tiam. Tiam himself fell ill with a persistent and enervating cough, at times expectorating blood. Eventually, under the doctor's care and with the support of Mae and Mrs. Watkins, Tiam seemed to recover fully.

To complicate matters, Mae became pregnant and the wedding date was abruptly pushed back.[21] The Watkinses engaged their Episcopal minister to officiate at the private ceremony to be held at the Watkins home on 12 September 1912. Tiam wired his father one last time. His father, Mr. Ng, wired back: "Must not marry." The next morning, the newlyweds woke to discover that their private wedding ceremony was front-page news in the Ann Arbor,

Grand Rapids, and Detroit papers. Some of the headlines and captions under both their pictures read: "U. of M. Co-Ed. Weds Chinese—News of Secret Wedding Startles Ann Arbor"; "U. of M. Stirred by Their Wedding"; "Ann Arbor Girl Weds Chinaman; Both Students—University City Stirred Up over Interracial Marriage of the Graduates—Efforts of Parents and Friends to Stop It Vain—Intimates of Bride Now Declare They Will Have Nothing More to Do with Her."

One article, "A Concrete Reason for the Race Prejudice at Ann Arbor," expressed concern that regardless of the happiness of the couple just married in Ann Arbor, their marriage would make it difficult to get students to attend the university, and "it is not unlikely when the news of the wedding is spread abroad more than one father and mother may hesitate to send their daughter to an institution which is likely to provide the young woman an Oriental husband as well as an education," the writer said.[22]

In response to the inaccuracies of these articles, Tiam wrote a letter to the editor of the *Ann Arbor Times,* published 15 September 1912, in which he cautioned the paper to get its facts straight. He also questioned the invasion of their privacy: "[Is] not the marriage confirmed with laws of both holy gospel and the land, and with the consent of the parents, as well as the parties—after all a private matter?" Tiam even listed his address and telephone number for anyone who cared to discuss the matter with him directly.

The times being what they were, however, Tiam and Mae felt forced to withdraw from the University of Michigan. Mae happily settled down at the Watkins home to prepare for the baby that was due in January. Tiam left for Detroit, where he found work at the Oriental Café. From there he kept in constant touch with Mae and the Watkins family. Soon he worked out his plans: "I don't care if I am a good waiter or not. All I want is a chance to get money and to complete my course of study." He then explained to Mae that he was happy that he had settled on a law career and had dropped the study of engineering. He would enroll at the Detroit College of Law immediately. Even with working part time at the café, he thought he could graduate in about a year (12 October 1912).

Tiam got off to a good start at Detroit with his instructors and classmates. Soon he was elected president of the Chinese Students' Alliance. But as well as things were going, Tiam knew that he could not practice law in the United States without being a citizen. He realized, too, that he could not give up his dream of returning to China to do what other returned students before him had done: work to infuse the old traditional country with the new blood of the West. Mae was filled both with excitement at the thought of seeing her husband's homeland and with pain at the thought of leaving her own. With the plans agreed upon, Tiam was happy. He made all the necessary contacts as he prepared to return to China through the auspices of the YMCA. He would work as a teacher in Shanghai until he could get a license to practice law from the government in Peking.

Tiam's joy intensified when Mrs. Watkins happily wrote to announce the birth of his son on 6 January 1913: "He's an old bouncer as we say when we mean a good sized child. And he looks like his papa. Both came through fine. Mae is resting comfortably." Tiam decided to call the boy Nelson, which meant "Right Obedience" in Chinese (10 January 1913).

The hard work and long hours finally paid off. "The degree title of Bachelor of Law is now mine," he wrote to Mae on 19 June 1913, his commencement day from the Detroit College of Law, "It [is] vested in me for all time." The note arrived with a bouquet of flowers.

Events moved rapidly after Tiam was graduated. By August his plans to return to China were finalized. By October he had earned enough money for passage to Shanghai and enough to support Mae and Nelson in the meantime. By November Tiam had departed for China. Mae had found it hard to part with him at the Ann Arbor depot. The frequent partings in the past now seemed to be merely rehearsals for this one. Neither the job contract in Shanghai, nor the train tickets to California, nor the packed bags loaded on the train prepared her to let him go at that very last minute.

The parting was equally hard for Tiam. He sent Mae a trail of postcards and hastily written letters from Colorado to California. From San Francisco, Tiam would sail on the Japanese steamer *Tenyo Maru* to Shanghai. Once in San Francisco at the Oriental Hotel on Stockton Street, Tiam had some time to explore Chinatown. He told Mae that it made him feel as if he were already back in China. "But I would rather be & see them in China where they would be entitled to full rights & privileges as citizens," he commented (7 December 1913).

The baby kept Mae occupied, but on the day that Tiam sailed, she wrote him that there was an added ache in her heart. Then she added hopefully: "God brot [sic] you to me once, halfway round the world, and I know he will guide me to you again" (16 December 1913).

Tiam's letters continued to arrive, but now they were posted from the Association Building at 120 Szechuen Road, Shanghai, China. Tiam taught fifteen hours a week at the YMCA and immediately applied to the Peking government for a license to practice law. As soon as he had time, Tiam began to search for a home for the family. That February, Tiam heard from one of his brothers, who told him that his parents were thinking about him all the time. And later that month, a letter arrived from Tiam's mother. She invited him to come home for a visit. "From the tone of her letter," Tiam wrote Mae, "I can make up with her easily, but she has to do what my father thinks" (22 February 1914).

In his 3 April 1914 letter, Tiam happily informed Mae that he had rented a newly built house for them. He would move in as soon as the lights and the gas stove were installed. "There are five rooms with a kitchen on the back over which [there is] a back porch for drying and a front porch for children to play," he noted. It was also in April that Mae could finally write Tiam a detailed letter about her own travel plans. She and Nelson would sail from Vancouver on 25 June on the *Empress of India* and would reach China on 14 July. In regard to his many plans, she added, "Be sure, dearest, that any arrangements you wish to make will be perfectly satisfactory to me. So long as you are my husband, all mine, I shall be happy" (28 April 1914).

Regret at leaving her family shadowed Mae's travel preparations. And some unpleasantness occurred when well-intentioned friends and relatives expressed concern about the kind of life that Mae would have in such a "heathen land." Mae had heard all that kind of talk before, but she knew that now it would upset her family just when they needed all their courage to let her and the baby go.

All fears vanished, however, when Mae wrote home that she and Nelson were safely and happily settled with Tiam in their first home at 39 Fu Teh Li, North Szechuen Road, Shanghai, China. "Dearest Mother, Dad & Gwen— Tiam had the house all arranged when we came. We have a maid and a nurse for Nelson" (24 July 1914). Thus began the first in a long series of detailed letters[23] that Mae wrote to her parents and sister, describing her life in China during World War I. Unfortunately, this first letter also contained the first intimation of trouble. "Everything is wonderful except Tiam has a cough. He says he's had it since he's been here. One doctor said it sounded more like bronchitis rather than tuberculosis" (24 July 1914).

By the end of the summer, the family was relatively settled. Mae encouraged Tiam to accept his mother's invitation home. When Tiam arrived in Amoy, he wrote to Mae that he was very happy that he had made the trip: "Everything is right at home now, except for them teasing me about building a big and larger house of foreign style in the settlement" (7 August 1914). At that same time, Tiam had resolved a legal dispute to everyone's satisfaction. He thought that this would cinch his chances of getting his legal license.

In several letters Mae tried to explain to her mother why she was not fully sympathetic to the English cause. Many of her reasons, she noted, she had learned in history classes at the University of Michigan. For one thing, she thought that England was trying to destroy Germany because Germany was becoming an economic threat to it. Mae warned: "Let me tell you a crushed and humiliated Germany will be a far greater menace to the peace of the world than a Germany left to pursue her legitimate way. . . . And where will be the gain to civilization when Russia, barbarous in the truer sense of the word spreads herself like 'an ulcer which leechcraft may not cure,' over the whole of Europe?" Furthermore, Mae objected to England's ally Japan, which was trying to "fill his precious fists with the coveted soil of China in spite of China's neutrality" (14 December 1914).[24]

The new year of 1915 got off to a fine start. Tiam was admitted to the Mixed Court of the International Settlement, which gave him the right to practice law in the U.S. courts as well as the others. Mae wrote her family about the plans to open a law college for the study of Chinese law that coming fall. Tiam was expected to have a share in that work, too (21 January 1915). Mae jotted this letter while her students at the Chinese girls' high school were taking a history examination.

Mae's happiness was abruptly shattered, however, when one of Tiam's lungs severely hemorrhaged. He was working too hard both at the National Institute at Woosung and at the Government Institute of Technology plus carrying on his law practice. She told her parents: "Of course I'm pretty much worried all the time now. Tiam probably has tuberculosis, tho if he is careful and has proper treatment there is no reason why he shouldn't get over it soon" (3 May 1915).

Tiam's health improved, and the family moved that September to a lovely brick house at 289 Avenue Joffre in the French Concession. He also opened a law office at 17 Nanking Road. A couple of months later, Mae announced that they were expecting their second child and described her plans to take Nelson and his *amah* with her to a Dr. Chang's house for the delivery. An attempt at a "third revolution" made it unsafe for her to go to the hospital, "which is unfortunately situated between the gunboats on the water and the arsenal on the shore" (20 December 1915). The letter home contained a birth announcement for Alason Franking, born 5 January 1916 and weighing eight pounds.

In February, Tiam found himself in Amoy again, presenting a case at the Mixed Court in the province of Kulangsu. "The civil governor at Fooshow has telegraphed to ask me [to visit], so I shall have to go to see him first on my way back after the trial." Tiam was to stay on to help celebrate his mother's birthday. "Perhaps I may bring four or five back with me including my mother to stay with us" (23 February 1916).

In the summer of 1916, Mae wrote to her parents that Tiam, who was supposed to be on vacation, "has a law case on one hand and on the other is preparing a text book on English composition for the college English classes. . . . Tiam will sell it outright to the publisher. It's less trouble than retaining the copyright ourselves." The publisher paid Tiam $200. Mae provided a couple of anecdotes, as she always did, about the boys. She was enjoying Nelson and Alason and expected "things will be superlatively exciting around here in a year or two." But she still keenly missed her family: "I dream time and time again that you have come here or I have gone there, and I talk myself hoarse every time. When I wake up, it always seems as tho I had been with you." She hoped that they would see each other in the not-too-distant future, but she said they all had a good laugh about the fortuneteller who had predicted to her mother that the Frankings would return to the United States in 1918 (25 July 1916).

In September, Mae sent word about her Chinese mother-in-law, who "is just as nice as ever—or I might say, nicer, because this time I wasn't as scared of her" (19 September 1916). She wanted to take Nelson and Alason back to Amoy for a visit. Mae hastily penned this letter between getting Tiam's book ready for the publishers and correcting seventy composition papers of her own students.

Mae and Tiam were happy with their lives in spite of their busy schedules: "The Dean of the Law School is going to America and has got Tiam to be acting dean in his place in addition to his regular teaching there and at the Government Institute of Technology," she explained to her family. "Then I have arranged to teach English three afternoons a week in the Nanyang Engineering and Mining College. I have also some idea of publishing another book entitled "Matrimonial Musings of G." (12 February 1917).

When her mother wrote expressing concern about Tiam's health, Mae responded that she was scared all the time about it, but took some consolation in comparing her fate to that of the war widows: "It seems to me that the woman whose husband is beside her . . . enjoys the most priceless blessing" (12 February 1917). Mae often told her mother about how happy she was with Tiam and her life. Sometimes they would not see each other all day: "But it happens that in going to the law school he travels for about a mile over the road by which I come home from school. So by watching closely for that distance I sometimes catch a glimpse of him for a second in passing. I always watch, and when I do see him, I am as delightfully happy as—well, as tho it were years ago in Ann Arbor and I was just beginning to suspect that I loved him. . . . Yet more so, I am happier than I ever was before in my life" (24 February 1917).

Tiam kept Mr. Rankin, the dean, posted on what was happening at the law school during his absence. In one letter he commented on the need for law schools in China that could make use of the excellent systematic work then being done in codifying and translating the body of Chinese law. Tiam told the dean: "Personally, I believe the comparative idea is practical & particularly valuable for with the growth of Republican ideals our western law has a part to play which cannot be overlooked." He then mentioned how this particular law school was a pioneer in the field of comparative law and that such schools would have great impact on China's government in the future. "The study of law is especially attractive to those who hope by judicial reform to make China a better example of representative government & to place China on equality with other nations in regard to international law," Tiam concluded (18 March 1917).

On 9 July 1917 Mae posted her last letter from 289 Avenue Joffre, Shanghai. It was filled with details of a dinner party they had given at the Astor House: "Entertained the Commissioner for Foreign Affairs, the judge of the United States Supreme Court for China, and some others." She noted that they had entertained former ambassadors, railway and college presidents, and the like. But she did not write about all that because she was not sure her folks would be interested.

By the following December, the Frankings were at Tiam's ancestral home in Amoy.[25] Mae, who had not wanted to worry her mother, gently broke the news of the birth of their third child, Cecile Mae Franking on 19 November. The child was born in Swatow on the family's journey south. Everyone was thrilled, since the family had many sons, but Cecile was the first girl born in two generations. Tiam's mother was carrying her around, showing her off to friends and neighbors, proud that she looked so much like Tiam when he was a baby. Unfortunately, Tiam himself was having a strenuous time for a man out in search of health" (18 December 1917).

Tiam left Amoy for Peking, and Mae found it terribly lonely without him. "I tell him his mother had just been able to really get acquainted with him for the first time since he left to go to the Philippines years and years ago, and so it is hard for her to lose him again," Mae wrote her parents. In that same letter, Mae described her father-in-law as being a nice papa who was "almost good enough for [Tiam's] mama." His manner was pleasing and not at all "bear-bitey" as she had imagined. She regretted that they could not converse because she had wasted time on Latin and German instead of learning Chinese and Spanish (20 March 1918).

Tiam wrote frequently to Mae from Peking, where he was hoping to be appointed to a government post. He tried to create the impression that he was rich and independent and could hold out for a "fat position." To be sent out as consul or mixed court magistrate, he needed to know the minister in the Office of Foreign Affairs. To be sent out as a judge, he needed to know the minister of justice. The place where he was staying reminded him of the dormitory for students in America, and he happily recalled his "student's days spirit of work & push." Tiam also mentioned that he read in the paper that a petition had been sent to the government to prohibit Chinese students abroad from marrying foreign wives. Even the secretary of the YMCA had questioned him about his marriage. Tiam added that he told him, "I couldn't get a better & happier wife. Shut his mouth" (12 March 1918).

By the end of April, Tiam felt less hopeful. He mentioned that he had given a number of dinner parties to men in positions to help him get an appointment. But he assured Mae that they entertained "in restaurants & without dames. . . . I can judge from their words & actions that they do not dare to get me into such social practice—much credit is due to you, dearest." It also eased Tiam's mind that Mae and the children were enjoying their days at his home in Amoy and "receiving attention due them," which he attributed to his parents and "not our marriage which attracts only curiosity & not substantial sympathy from outside." He added that a Mr. Chu had spent $1,500 in order to become the commissioner of foreign affairs: "Oh, it is such a rotten place, but that is the spirit of the politics here." He closed with "Dearest, I am with you, do you feel it? With love, Tiam" (30 April 1918).

Finally, Tiam wrote telling Mae that it looked as if he would have to take a position at the consulate-general's office in San Francisco, which only paid about $150 a month (15 May 1918). In mid-December, Mae wrote to her family from the consulate-general's office at 617 Montgomery Street, San Francisco, that they were "hereby officially informed that they had arrived on Friday, Dec. 13, 1918, on the T.K.K. S.S. 'Siberia Maru' from Amoy, China via Hong Kong, Shanghai, Nagasaki, Kobe, Yokohama, and Honolulu." Mae also pointed out that when she first sailed for China the shot that started World War I had just been fired and on her return voyage the war had ended: "Makes me feel as big as the wind when he blew out the moon." Mae, however, forgot about the fortuneteller who had predicted their return in 1918 (15 December 1918).

The Frankings arrived safely, but at a time when San Francisco was "caught in the whirl of a second epidemic" of influenza. Mae was ill for awhile, then

Tiam caught it. By February 1919, Tiam had been confined to bed for two weeks with two doctors attending him. The last one diagnosed him as having bronchial pneumonia, coupled with a mild case of influenza. This doctor also detected some tubercular "bugs" in the specimens he gave to the laboratory. "I guess he has never been so sick before. . . . You would feel sad to see how thin & weak he is. But the hardest part seems to be over," Mae told her family, "and we all feel that he is getting better now" (19 February 1919).

By that March, Tiam, who was twenty-nine, had died. His body was returned to Amoy for burial. Mae's intense personal grief was eased somewhat by her firm spiritual belief that she and Tiam would be joined as husband and wife in a life beyond.

Thus end the events covered in *My Chinese Marriage*. As a brief epilogue for those interested, Mae went back with her three children to Ann Arbor, where she lived with her parents. Her sister, Gwen, was married by then and expecting a child of her own, a daughter, Marilyn. Later she also had a son. Mae contracted tuberculosis herself shortly after completing her manuscript. She spent two years in a TB sanitorium but was able to return home to be with her parents and three children when she died in 1926 at the age of thirty-five. Years later Mae's daughter, Cecile, would write a short story about the day that she and the others learned from the doctor that Mae did not have long to live.[26]

After Mae's death, Tiam's parents sent a member of the clergy to request that the grandchildren return to China to live with them. Nelson, who was thirteen years old at the time, had to make the decision for himself and his brother and sister. He decided that it was best that they stay in Ann Arbor with Gram and Dad Watkins. Mae's sister, Gwen, died in 1985, at the age of eighty-five. Mr. Watkins died of cancer while in his sixties, but his wife lived on well into her eighties. She saw Mae and Tiam's children grown and most of them married. She even lived to see the birth of her first great-granddaughter, Marilyn Ann, born to Alason and Phyllis Franking in 1940. They also have a son, Neal. Nelson and Elizabeth O'Connor Franking have three children: Ronald, Holly, and Michael. Nelson died in 1979; he is buried in Ann Arbor next to his mother and grandparents. Like her parents, Cecile met her husband, William Q. Wu, who was a medical student from mainland China, while both were studying at the University of Michigan. The two became citizens of the United States. The Wus have two sons, William Franking and Christopher Nelson.

Mae Franking's
My Chinese Marriage

I

IN AMERICA

I saw Chan-King Liang[1] for the first time on a certain Monday morning in October. It was the opening day of college,[2] and the preceding week had been filled with the excitement incidental to the arrival of many students in a small town[3] given over to family life. Every household possessed of a spare room was impressed with the fact that good citizenship demanded that it harbor a student. Therefore, when I saw trunks and boxes and bags being tumbled upon the front porch of our next-door neighbor, I said to Mother,[4] "Mrs. James has succumbed!" and set out for my first class with Celia, an old friend.

As we crossed the campus, we noticed a group of boys, gathered on the steps of College Hall and talking among themselves. Celia turned to me. "Do you see the one with very black hair, his face turned away a little—the one in the gray suit, Margaret?[5]—Well, that is the new Chinese student, and the boys all say he is a wonder. My cousin knew him last year in Chicago, where he was a freshman. Going in for international law and political science—imagine!"

I turned and glanced with a faint interest at the foreign student, on whose black hair the sun was shining. My first impression was of a very young, smiling lad. "Looks well enough," I said, rather ungraciously, and we passed on.

I was a busy student, eagerly beginning my freshman year's work, and I thought no more of the young Chinese. But a day or so later I discovered him to be the owner of those trunks and bags I had seen assembled on Mrs. James' porch. Chan-King was my next-door neighbor.

We were never introduced to each other, as it happened, and, though we shared studies in German and French, we did not exchange a word for some time. Later I found myself admiring his feat of learning two foreign languages through the medium of English, a third, and doing it so very well. At the same time, though I was not then aware of the fact, he was also admiring me for proficiency in these subjects, in which I was working hard, because I intended to teach languages.

The progress of my interest in him was gradual and founded on a sense of his complete remoteness, an utter failure to regard him as a human being like the rest of us. He was the first of his race I had ever seen. But finally we spoke to one another by some chance, and, after that, it seemed unnecessary to refuse to walk to class with him on a certain morning when we came out of our houses at the same moment.

We parted at College Hall door with an exchange of informal little nods. I was happily impressed, but my impulse to friendship suffered a quick reaction from all that Chan-King was, when viewed against the background of his race as I saw it. I had no intention whatever of continuing our association.

Naturally, Chan-King knew nothing of this. I think I was probably a trifle more courteous to him than was necessary. I remember being uneasy for fear of wounding him by some thoughtless remark that would reveal my true state of mind about China. I lost sight of the race in the individual. I even pretended not to notice that he was waiting for me morning after morning when I emerged, always a trifle late, hurrying to classes. By the close of the first semester, we were making the trip together almost daily as a matter of course.

He was gay and friendly, with a sort of frank joyousness that was his own special endowment for living. I enjoyed his companionship, his talk, his splendid spirit. His cheerfulness was a continual stimulant to my moody, introspective, static temperament. I used to study his face, which in repose had the true oriental impassivity—a stillness that suggested an inner silence or brooding. But this mood was rare in those days, and I remember best his laughter, his shining eyes that never missed the merriment to be had from the day's routine events.

For a while we were merely two very conventional young students walking sedately together, talking with eagerness on what now seem amusingly sober and carefully chosen subjects. We were both determined to be dignified and impersonal. I was nineteen, and Chan-King was two years older.

Finally, Chan-King asked to call and he appeared at the door that evening, laden with an enormous, irregular package, a collection of treasures that he thought might interest us. We all gathered about the library table, where he spread a flaming array of embroidered silks, carved ivory and sandalwood and curious little images in bronze and blackwood. They gave out a delicious fragrance, spicy and warm and sweet, with a bitter tang to it, a mingling of oils and lacquers and dust of incense.

He was very proud of half a dozen neckties his mother had made him, patterned carefully after the American one he had sent her as a souvenir. "She sews a great deal, and everything she does is beautiful," he said, stroking one of the ties, fashioned of wine-colored silk and embroidered in a thin gold thread.

The simple words, the tangle of the exotic things lying on the table, in that moment set the whole world between us. I saw him as alien, far removed and unknowable; I realized how utterly transplanted he must be, moving as he did in a country whose ideals, manners and customs must appear, at times, grotesquely fantastic to him. "How queer we must seem to you!" I exclaimed, impulsively, lifting a solid, fat little idol in my hand.

"Queer? Not at all—but wonderfully interesting in everything. You see, to me it is all one world!" Our eyes met for a second. Then he offered me a small embroidered Chinese flag. I hesitated, looking at the writhing, fire-breathing dragon in many-colored silks. Again the old prejudice swept over me. I was about to refuse. But I saw in his eyes an expression of hesitating, half-anxious pleading, which touched me. I took the flag, puzzled a trifle over that look I had surprised.

Chan-King became a frequent visitor at our home in the evenings, making friends with my father and mother, with true Chinese deference. I like to remember those times, with all of us sitting around the big table, the shaded lamp casting a clear circle of light on the books and papers, the rest of the room in pleasant dimness. It was during these evenings that Chan-King told us about his father, typical Chinese product of his clan and time, who had early perceived the limitations of a too nationalistic point of view and had planned western education for his sons, of whom Chan-King was the eldest. From his talk I reconstructed a half-picture of his home in southern China.[6] It was a large household of brothers and relatives and servants ruled over by his mother during the prolonged absences of his father, whose business interests lay in a far-away island port.[7]

Once he brought a faded photograph of a small boy formally arrayed in the Chinese velvets and satins of an earlier period. "Myself at the age of six," he explained.

I examined the picture closely. "Why, Mr. Liang," I said, in wonder, "you are wearing a—wearing a—queue!"

He smiled, delighted at my confusion. "Yes, a very nice queue it was," he declared, "bound with a scarlet silk cord. I remember how it waved in the wind when I flew my kite on the hills!"

"You wore a black queue yourself, Margaret," interposed my mother, her eyes twinkling, "shorter than this, but often tied with a red silk ribbon."

"You see, we had that in common, at least," said Chan-King. And he flashed a grateful smile at mother. There was a well-established friendship between my kindly, understanding mother and Chan-King while my feeling for him was still uncertain.

Yet in spite of all these reasons for close sympathy with Chan-King, I felt toward him at times something amounting almost to dislike. Against such states of mind my sense of personal justice, a trait I had directly from my Scotch inheritance, instantly rebelled. I was careful in no way to reveal my feelings, though I probably should have done so had I even remotely realized that friendship was verging upon love. As it was, I had an ideal of genuine comradeship, of a pleasant interlude destined to end with our college days.

Toward the end of the winter, as our acquaintance advanced, there came to me a series of those revulsions. I assured myself that so ephemeral a relation as ours must be was hardly worth the time I was giving to it. I remembered that, fine as Chan-King was, he belonged to the Chinese race. I decided to put an end to the entire episode at once. The way in which I carried out this plan was unnecessarily abrupt. I avoided him, unmistakably, going to class and returning home by a roundabout way, and refusing to see him either in class or on the campus.

Then, one afternoon at the end of two weeks, he was waiting for me before the main door of College Hall. I did not speak. He joined me without a word and walked in silence to the campus edge. I turned suddenly toward a side street. "Go that way if you like," I said, rudely. "I have an errand this way."

He came with me. "I wish to talk with you," he said, with an oddly restrained, patient tone of weariness. Our eyes met, and I saw in his a gentle and touching determination to understand and be understood, which would have been more significant to me if I had been less engrossed in my own emotions.

"Why do you wish to end our friendship?" he asked, quietly, with his characteristic frankness.

"I—because I thought it was best," I stammered, completely disarmed.

"It is never best to give up a friendship," he said. "But it happens that our friendship may end soon after all. It is possible I shall return to China. To-day I received a cablegram from my father, saying my mother is dangerously ill. I shall know within a day or so whether I am to go or to stay."

Human sympathy triumphed over race prejudice. "Come home with me," I said, "and let mother talk to you. She always knows what to say."

Another cablegram two days later brought the good news of his mother's improvement. Chan-King's anxiety during those two days wrung me. He said nothing, but his face was strained and lined. He walked and we talked a good deal of other things, and he gave me definite outlines of his "life-plan," as he called it. He regarded the diplomatic service of his country as his final goal, but, on the way to it, he wished to take part in constructive teaching and sociological work in China. He was keenly enthusiastic about the ancient arts and natural beauties of China and venerated many of her old customs. "I hope introducing modern education will not destroy the beauty of the East," he told me, but he was solidly convinced of the need for new ideas in all the Orient. I began to see his country through new eyes.

We were soon going about together a great deal. I remember many happy parties on the lantern-lighted campus, many field-days and tennis matches, all the innocent freedom of college life that we enjoyed together. I was rather remote in my personal friendships, and very little was said to me regarding my association with the Chinese student. But now I began to hear small murmurs, a vague hum of discussion, and to observe an interested watching of us by the students and townspeople. I could not help seeing that curious glances followed us when we entered a tea-room or concert hall together.

Several friends of my mother's spoke disapprovingly to her of the matter. "What if they should fall in love—marry?" asked one conventional-minded old lady. But my mother was born without prejudices and never sees boundary lines or nationalities. She was infinitely tactful and kind. I know now that she was rather uneasy, for she felt that marriage is a difficult enough relation when each person knows the other's heritage and formulas; but she said nothing to make me self-conscious, not even repeating the remarks of her acquaintances until long afterward.

However, I heard comments from other sources, which irritated me a trifle and had the perfectly natural effect of stimulating my loyalty to Chan-King and arousing at times a yearning tenderness to shield him from injustice. At this time we tentatively expressed our views on inter-marriage. We were sitting on the porch late one afternoon. "I believe marriage between alien races is a mistake," I said, in the decisive way I cultivated at that time. "It is better to marry one's own kind."

"No doubt there are fewer difficulties," he answered, without conviction. "It is all so much a personal problem. Marriages between Americans do not seem to be always successful."

I flared. "We hear only of the unhappy ones," I retorted.

"But there are many, many unhappy ones, then," he returned gently. "I wonder if unhappy marriage in all countries is not due to selfishness and lack of love and to unwillingness to compromise on unimportant differences."

We could not possibly quarrel here, and our talk proceeded amiably.

My thoughts at dinner that night seem very amusing to me as I recall them now. Chan-King was so like one of us, as we sat at table together, that I found myself wondering if it was true that a Chinese wife did not eat at the same table with her husband; if she actually did wait upon him and obey him without question in everything; if Chan-King would return to China soon and there become an insufferable, autocratic eastern husband. The thought oppressed me unbearably. Since Chan-King was leaving next day on a summer-vacation trip, this was a farewell dinner. He insisted on helping me with the dishes afterward, for ours was a simple household, and we usually had no maid. We were very merry over the task. "In China," he confided, as he stacked the saucers, "the lot of women is much easier. They have servants for everything of this kind. I know an Englishwoman who married a Chinese, and she afterward taught in a college for the sake of something to do."

"She did quite right," I said. "Idleness is not good for anyone."

"Chinese wives are not idle," he answered, gravely; "they have many duties for everyone in their household."

At this he turned his eyes upon me, with an intent, inner look. Because I was impressed, I chose to be flippant.

"If I obstruct your view, I will move," I said.

"It would do no good," he answered. "You are always there—wherever I want to look."

Later he was writing his name in Chinese characters on a photograph he had given my mother. I stood beside him. He dropped the pen, turned to me and took both my hands in his own. He bent toward me, and I drew away, shaking my head decisively. I wrenched one hand free, and the kiss he meant for my lips reached my fingers instead. I was overwhelmed with a sense of invasion. We quarreled, but without bitterness or real anger. I was simply convinced that, since love was not for us, we were bound by all ethics to keep our relations in the outward seeming of friendship. For a moment I felt that one of my ideals had been rudely shattered.

"Oh, but you have mistaken me!" he declared, earnestly, refusing to release my hand.

"Kisses are not for friendship," I managed to say.

"I'm sorry," he confessed, but I saw in his eyes that he regretted my misunderstanding of him, nothing more.

During his summer travels he wrote me many letters. I had time to think, and in my thoughts I admitted that to be a friend to Chan-King was better than to have the love of anyone else in the world.

When he returned, we wandered together one evening down to the campus and sat on a stone bench in the moon-shade of a tall tree. I had overheard a remark, tinged with race prejudice, that had awakened again in my heart that brooding maternal tenderness, and when Chan-King's eyes pleaded wistfully, I gave him, as a sacrificial offering, the kiss before denied.[8]

That fall he transferred for a year to a New England university.[9] He told me long afterward it was so that absence might teach me to know my own heart. I loved him now and admitted it to myself with bitter honesty.[10] But all fulfillment of love seemed so hopeless and remote, the chasm fixed between our races seemed so impassable, that I gave up in my heart and put away his letters as they came, smiling with affected youthful cynicism at the memory of that kiss, which could mean nothing more to us than a sweet and troubled recollection.

He came back unexpectedly at the end of the college term.[11] There was an indescribably hopeful, anxious look in his eyes as he took my hands. My first sight of his face, grown older and graver in those long months, brought a shock of poignant happiness, very near to tears. Off guard, we met as lovers, with all antagonisms momentarily swept away, all pretenses forgotten. I went to his arms as my one sure haven. For this hour love made everything simple and happy.

My father and mother were astonished when we told them of our intention to marry.[12] With gentle wisdom, mother suggested that we allow ourselves a year of engagement, "in order to be sure," as she expressed it. We were very sure but we consented.

Chan-King wrote at once to his people in south China, telling of his engagement. For me, he had one important explanation, made in his frank, straightforward way. "In China," he told me, "it is usual for parents to arrange their children's marriages, often years in advance. When I was very young, it was generally understood that I would later marry the daughter of my father's good friend, three years younger than I. There was no formal betrothal, and, when I left home to study, I asked my father not to make any definite plans for my marriage until my return. The subject has never been mentioned since, and I don't know what his ideas are now. But they can make no difference with us— you understand that, Margaret, dear?" Again I felt myself in spiritual collision with unknown forces and wondered at his calmness in opposing the claims of his heredity.

His family replied to his letter with a cablegram, forbidding the marriage. I had never seriously expected any other decision. A letter followed, conciliatory in tone, in which his father explained that since Chan-King's foreign education was nearly completed, arrangements had been made for his marriage to Miss Li-Ying immediately upon his return home. He gave a charming description of his bride, whom Chan-King had not seen for twelve years. She was, he said, young and modest and kind, she was beautiful and wealthy, and moreover had been given a modern education in order to fit her for the position of wife to an advanced Chinese. The match was greatly desired by both families. In conclusion, the letter urgently requested that Chan-King would not make it impossible for his father to fulfill the contract he had entered into with a friend, and very gently intimated that by doing so he would forfeit all right to further consideration.

There were other letters. An American friend, a missionary, wrote—oh, very tactfully—of the difficulties he would have in keeping an American wife happy in the Orient. A Chinese cousin discussed at length the sorrows a foreign daughter-in-law would bring into his house—the bitterness of having in the family an alien and stubborn woman, who would be unwilling to give his parents the honor due them or to render them the service they would expect of their son's wife.

Many letters of this kind came in a group. There was a hopeless tone of finality, a solid clan consciousness in those letters that frightened me a little. I was uneasy, uncertain. I had found no irreconcilable elements in our minds, for I was very conservative West, and he was very liberal East. But here were represented the people with whom his life must be spent and the social background against which it must harmoniously unfold. I felt with terrific force that it was not Chan-King, but Chan-King's traditions and ancestors, his tremendous racial past, that I must reckon with.

Also, I did not wish to stand in the way of his future. I doubt if I could have found courage to marry Chan-King, if I had then realized the importance—especially in diplomatic and political circles—of clan and family influence in China. But he gave it up so freely, with such assured and unregretful cheerfulness, that I could not but share his mood.

In these calm, logical, impersonal family letters, which Chan-King translated for me, there was a strain of sinister philosophy that chilled me as I read. The letters dealt entirely with his duty in its many phases—to his parents, to his ancestors, to his country, to his own future. Nothing of love! Only one relative—a cousin—mentioned it at all, and in this wise: "You are young now, and to youth love seems of great importance. But as age replaces youth, you will find that love runs away like water."

"That is not true, Chan-King," I said, with solemn conviction. "Love is greater than life or age; it lives beyond death. It is love that makes eternity!"

At this time, Chan-King did not quite comprehend my mystical interpretation of love. But he answered very happily, "To have you for my wife is worth everything else the world can offer."

Chan-King continued to write to his family briefly and respectfully, declining to be influenced in any way. Replies came at lengthening intervals and then ceased. There was no open breach, no violent tearing asunder of bonds. Courteously, quite gently, the hands of his people were removed, and he stood alone.[13]

"But surely your mother will not give you up!" I exclaimed one day when it dawned on me that not one message had she sent in all the correspondence.

"Not in her dear heart," he said, with unshaken faith, "but of course she will not write to me if my father disapproves."

"But a mother, Chan-King!" I protested. "Surely her feelings come first always!"

Chan-King's tone was patient after the manner of one who has explained an obvious fact many times. "In China," he reminded me again, "the family comes always before the individual. But with you and me, Margaret beloved, love has first importance."

His never-failing insistence upon viewing ours as an individual instance, not to be judged by any ordinary standards, was a source of great strength to me always. During the short period that followed before our marriage, we tiffed a few times in the most conventional manner, with fits of jealousy that had no foundation: small distrusts that on my part were merely efforts to uphold what I considered my proper feminine pride, and on his, were often failures to discount this characteristic temper of mine. Only, somehow, there was never any rancor in our quarrels. Not once would we deny our love for each other.[14]

So we planned to be married immediately. There were no reasons why we should delay further. That is to say, none but practical reasons, and what have they to do with young people in love? "It is a little late for us to begin practical thinking," said Chan-King cheerfully, when we discussed ways and means. "But we might as well make the experiment."

Chan-King was no longer merely a student with a generous allowance from a wealthy father.[15] On his own resources, with his education not completed, he was about to acquire a foreign wife and to face an untried world. We were strangely light-hearted about all this. Chan-King had regularly put by more than half his allowance since coming to America. I meant to be a teacher of languages, economically independent if circumstances required such aid for a man beginning a career. Our plans were soon completed. At the end of another term, which we would finish together, Chan-King would be graduated, and then, after a year of practice in his profession, he would return to China, there to begin his life work. I was to follow later. Nothing could have been more delightfully simple so far as we could see. A few days later we were married in my mother's house by an Anglican clergyman.[16] "Of course you will live here with us until you go to China," my parents had said. "We want our children with us, if you can be happy here."

This seemed a very natural arrangement to Chan-King, accustomed as he was to family life. But I was apprehensive. The popular western idea that people cannot be friends if they are related by law was heavy on my mind. I did not expect any drastic readjustment of temperament between my Chinese husband and me, but I did look forward somewhat timorously to a trying period of small complications due to differences in domestic customs and the routine of daily living.

I need not have worried a moment; a wonderful spirit of family coöperation was an important part of Chan-King's oriental heritage. From the day of our wedding[17] he took his place with charming ease and naturalness as a member of the household. The affection that existed between my husband and my parents simplified that phase of our relation perfectly, and left us free to adjust ourselves to each other and the world, though the latter we took very little into account. Until I met Chan-King, the idea of being conspicuous was unendurable to me. But when I early perceived that to appear with him anywhere was to invite the gaze of the curious, I discovered with surprise that it mattered not at all. I was very proud of my husband and loved to go about with him. We were happy from the beginning.

Discovering life together proved a splendid adventure, which renewed itself daily. The deep affection and tenderness between us created subtle comprehensions too delicate to be put into words. A quick look interchanged during a pause in talk would often convey a complete thought. I always felt that Chan-King had acuter perceptions, more reserve, and more imagination than I. Also he was meticulous—as I was not—in regard to small amenities. I had always been used to having my own way without causing discomfort to anyone else, but I found that I could not speak carelessly or act thoughtlessly without the risk of violating his sense of the fitness of things. My greatest difficulty in the first few months of our marriage[18] came from my constant effort to adjust my mode of thought and action to meet a highly trained and critical temperament, to whom the second-bests of association, spiritual or mental or material, were not acceptable. Yet, if he exacted much, he gave more. In everything, he had a generosity so sincere and spontaneous that it aroused a like quality in me.

I am in many ways the elemental type of woman, requiring, I know, a certain measure of domination in love. It was imperative that I respect my husband, and it pleased me to discover, in our several slight domestic crises, that his was far the stronger will. I had taken my vow to obey, having specified that the word was not to be omitted from the marriage ceremony.[19] How I should have kept it under a tyrannical will I do not know, for Chan-King was not a domestic dictator. He took it for granted that we were partners and equals in our own departments of life. He trusted my judgment in the handling of my share of our affairs, and in later years often came to me for advice in his own. Nevertheless, morally, the balance of power was in his hands, and I was glad to leave it there. Often our disagreements would end in laughter because each one of us would give way gradually from the position first assumed, until we had almost changed sides in the discussion. This happened again and again.

From the very beginning, I saw clearly, by some grace, the point at which Chan-King's oriental mind and occidental education came into the keenest conflict: my attitude toward other men and their attitude toward me. He was never meanly jealous or suspicious, but there was in him that unconquerable eastern sense of exclusiveness in love, that cherishing of personal possession, so incomprehensible to the average western imagination.

I had planned to instruct a young man in French during the summer months, as a part of my vacation work, and I casually announced my intention to Chan-King. He opposed it at once, I thought unfairly. I was a great while persuading him to admit his real reasons for objecting. Finally I said, somewhat at random, "If my pupil were a girl, you would not care."

"You have enough work as it is," he persisted, but without firmness, and his eyes flickered away from mine. I laughed a little. He turned to me a face so distressed that my smile died suddenly. "Oh, don't laugh!" he said, painfully in earnest. "You must keep in mind what you are to me. I—cannot be different. I am sorry."

I gave up my harmless young pupil and said nothing more. From that moment I began to form my entire code of conduct where men were concerned on a rigidly impersonal and formal basis. It was not difficult, for my first and only affection was centered in my husband, and the impulse to coquetry was foreign to my nature.

My husband's determination to leave my individuality untrammeled was sometimes overborne, in small ways that delighted me, by his innate sense of fitness. We played tennis and he played excellently. One day, as we left the courts, he said to me, "Tennis just isn't your game, Margaret. Your dignity is always getting in the way of your drive. I don't want you to give up your dignity—it is too much a part of you. But you might leave tennis alone and try archery. I am sure that is more suited to your type." The amused obedience with which I took his suggestion soon became enthusiasm for the new sport.

To me, marriage had always seemed the most mystic and important of human relations, involving at times all the rest—and particularly parenthood. I am a born mother, to whom the idea of marriage without children is unthinkable. Since I put away my dolls, dream children had taken their place in the background of my fancy. I saw them vaguely at first, but with the coming of love I knew quite clearly how they would look. Now that I had married Chan-King, I should have liked a child at once as a surer bond between us and a source of comfort for myself while he should be making his start in China. I knew that he loved children, for on several occasions I had deliberately put a tiny neighbor in his way and had taken note of his warm friendliness and gentleness with the wee thing. But, fearing that he would be unwilling to accept a new responsibility while our affairs were still unsettled, I put aside my desire for a child, though my loved books were growing strangely irksome. I did not know that my husband shared the usual foreign belief that the American woman is an unwilling mother.

Then one day he went to call on a friend of his, a Chinese student whose wife and little son were with him. "I saw the Chinese baby," he told me with boyish eagerness. "He is going to have a little brother soon. Lucky baby!"

"Lucky parents!" I corrected him, and sighed enviously. Chan-King looked at me, the wonder on his face growing into a delighted smile. "Do you mean it, Margaret?" he asked incredulously. Then we talked long and earnestly of our children. To Chan-King's old-world mind, children should follow marriage as naturally as fruit the blossom, and his happiness in discovering that my ideals were exactly his own brought us to another plane of understanding and contentment with each other. Besides, he explained, a grandchild would do much to reconcile his parents to our marriage.

Happily, when the school term was over, I put aside my books for a needle. I had always been fond of sewing, but never had I found such fascinating work as the making of those tiny garments of silk and flannel and lawn. My practical mother protested against so much embroidering, but my husband only smiled as he rummaged gently through the basket of small sewing.

"You are a real Chinese wife, after all," he would say. "A Chinese wife sews and embroiders a great deal. She even makes shoes for the family."

"Shoes, Chan-King?"

"Shoes, no less. To make shoes beautifully is a fine art, and a Chinese woman takes pride in excelling at it. She is proud of her feet and makes all her own slippers."

Then he would tell me stories of his childhood and recall memories of the closed garden in his old home, where he played at battledore with a tiny girl, while her mother and his mother sat together, embroidering and talking in low tones. The two young mothers were friends and were planning for the marriage of their son and daughter, which would strengthen the friendship into a family bond.

I took great interest in this little girl, who flitted through Chan-King's stories like a brilliant butterfly seen through a mist. Her name was Li-Ying and she was only three years old when she ran, with her little feet still unbound, through those sweetly remembered green gardens of his childhood. Somewhere now she was sitting, her lily feet meekly crossed, embroidering shoes, waiting until her father should betroth her to another youth.

When Chan-King showed me a portrait of himself, taken in a group with his mother and father when he was eight years old, I examined very thoughtfully the austerely beautiful face of the woman who had brought him into life.[20] She sat on one side of the carved blackwood table. Her narrow, paneled skirt was raised a trifle to show her amazingly tiny feet. On the other side of the table sat Chan-King's father, an irreconcilably stern and autocratic-looking man, magnificently garbed in the old style. Beside him stood a small, solemn boy, wearing a round cap, his queue still bound, he told me, with a red cord, his hands lost in the long velvet sleeves that reached almost to his knees. I put my finger on the head of this boy. "I hope our son will look exactly like him," I said.

At last the hoped-for son was born and laid in my arms.[21] He was swaddled and powdered and new and he wept for obscure reasons. But my husband and I smiled joyfully at the delicious, incredible resemblance of that tiny face to his own. Chan-King looked at him a long time, a quizzical, happy smile in the corners of his mouth. Then he kissed me very gently and said, "He's a real Liang baby, Margaret. Are you glad?" I answered that I was glad, as I had been for everything love had brought to me.

Our plans progressed favorably, and, when our son Wilfred[22] was five months old, Chan-King returned to China.[23] I told him good-by in the way I knew would please him most—calmly and without tears. But when it came to the last moment, I felt unable to let him go. Mutely I clung to him, the baby on my arm between us.

"It won't be for long, this," he assured me. "We shall all be together at home very soon. You are brave and dear and true, Margaret. You shall never be made sorry. Be patient."[24]

His first letters told of his new work in one of the older colleges for which Shanghai is famous.[25] He also began his practice of law[26] in an official capacity. His first step toward the diplomatic service had been taken.

At the end of four months, I received his summons and went about making ready for the journey to China with my young son.[27] My life-work was to help my husband in making a home. His life-work was in China. The conclusion was so obvious that neither I nor my parents had ever questioned it. But now that the moment had come, the friends of the family were very much excited. They asked strange questions. Are you really going? How can you leave your mother? How can you give up beautiful America? Aren't you afraid to go to China? I answered as patiently and reasonably as I could. They wearied me very much.

Of China itself I had no clear conception, in spite of Chan-King's letters, for though my old prejudice had passed away, yet still I saw all the country only as a background for my husband's face.

I followed Chan-King's minute instructions concerning traveling arrangements, and Wilfred and I had a pleasant voyage.[28] Early one morning I looked through the porthole and saw about me the murky waters of the Yangtze, alive with native craft, while dimly through the mist loomed the fortifications of Woosung. Already the tender was waiting, and soon we were aboard, moving rapidly up the mouth of the river. The mist cleared, green banks arose on each side, and through distant trees gleamed red brick buildings like any at home, side by side with the white-plastered walls and tip-tilted roofs of China. In that long ride, Shanghai grew upon me gradually, a curious mixture of the known and the unknown, tantalizing me with the feeling that I had seen all this before and ought to remember it better. In the water about me, steamer, launch and battle-ship mingled with native junk, river-barge and house-boat. Suddenly in the waiting group on the customs jetty I saw my husband. In another moment we had drawn alongside the wharf and he was in the tender beside me, greeting me in the formally courteous manner he deemed suited to public occasions. Taking Wilfred in his arms, he drew me up the steps and to a waiting carriage.

Here again was the confused mingling of the strange and the familiar: clanging tram-cars, honking automobiles, smooth-rolling rickshaws, creaking wheel-barrows and lumbering, man-drawn trucks; dark coolie-faces under wide straw hats, gently bred features beneath pith helmets, black, bearded countenances below huge, gay turbans; a bewildering jumble of alien and English speech.

Even in Chan-King I found it. He was wearing American dress, his face had not changed, the tones of his voice were the same, but he was speaking Chinese, and his directions to the *mafoo* were to me a meaningless succession of sounds.

But when he was beside me in the carriage and the horses had started, he turned suddenly and smiled straight into my eyes. Then, Shanghai, Borneo or the North Pole—all would have been one to me. I asked no questions; I was with my husband and child, driving rapidly toward the home prepared for me. I had come home to China.

I I

IN SHANGHAI

My first impressions of Shanghai are a blur. My husband and I drove rapidly along the Bund, over Garden Bridge, which might have been any bridge in America, past the Astor House, which was very like any American hotel, and then along the Soochow Creek, which could be only in China.

On North Szechuan Road we stopped at a *li,* or terrace, of newly built houses in the style called semi-foreign. This *li,* which was in the International Settlement, was very bright and clean. It opened upon the main thoroughfare. The heavy walls of bright red brick were interrupted at intervals by black doors bearing brass name-plates. At one of these my husband stopped and touched a very American-looking push-button. A bell trilled within, and the door was opened by a smiling "boy" in a long blue cotton gown. We crossed a small courtyard bright with flowers and vines, and, coming to the main entrance, stepped directly into a large square room. It was cool, immaculate and restful. The matting-covered floors, the skillfully arranged tables, chairs and sofa, the straight hangings of green and white, threaded with gold, were exactly what I should have wished to choose for myself. I was pleasantly surprised by the gas chandelier with its shades of green and gold and white. A dark green gas radiator along one wall suggested that Shanghai was not always so warm as then. It was a very modest little home, befitting a man with his own way to make, Chan-King explained, as he led me through the rooms for a hasty survey. Then Wilfred was surrendered to his *amah,* a fresh-cheeked young woman in stiffly starched blue "coat," white trousers and apron, while we made ready for a tiffin engagement with Chinese friends of Chan-King's.

After a short rickshaw ride—novel and delightful to me—we turned from the main road into another series of terraces and entered a real Chinese household. The host and hostess, who had both been in America and spoke excellent English, were very cordial in their welcome. I felt more at home than I had believed could be possible. Tiffin was served in the Chinese fashion, the guests seated at a great round table, with the dishes of meat, fish and vegetables placed in the center, so that each one could help himself as he chose. Individual bowls of rice, small plates, chopsticks and spoons were at each plate. Set at intervals, were small, shallow dishes containing soy, mustard or catsup and also roasted melon-seeds and almonds. When my hostess, who had thoughtfully rounded out her delicious Chinese menu with bread and butter and velvety ice-cream, as thoughtfully produced a silver knife and fork for me, my husband explained that I was rather deft in the use of chopsticks. Though he had taught me, during the early days of our marriage, to use a slender ivory pair that he possessed, I was now very nervous, but I felt obliged to prove his delighted assertion. So my social conformity as a Chinese wife began there, before a friendly and amused audience, who assured me that I did very well.

On the way home Chan-King said, "Will this be difficult for you, Margaret?"

"Chopsticks?" I asked gaily, well enough knowing that he did not mean chopsticks. "No, I like them!"

"I mean everything," he said very gravely, "China—customs, people, homesickness, everything."

"You will see whether you haven't married a true Oriental," I answered him. "As for homesickness, why, Chan-King—I am at home."

The most important thing at first, materially speaking, was that Chan-King must make his own way without help of any sort. And for the upper class Chinese this is very difficult. He was teaching advanced English in one of the largest colleges in Shanghai, maintaining a legal practice and giving lectures on international law. He was glad to be at home again, filled with enthusiasm for his work, hopeful as the young returned students always are at first, and, through sheer inability to limit his endeavors, working beyond his strength.

Our happiness at being together again made all things seem possible. From its fragmentary beginnings in America, we gathered again into our hands the life we expected to make so full and rich. My part, I recognized, was to be a genuinely old-fashioned wife—the rôle I was best fitted for, and the one most helpful to Chan-King. And I began by running my Chinese household with minute attention to providing for his comfort in small ways that he liked and never failed to appreciate.

Our two-story house consisted of two big rooms downstairs and sleeping apartments and a tiny roof-garden upstairs.[1] In this roof-garden I spent most of my time, and there Wilfred and his *amah* passed many afternoons. It was a pleasant, sunny place, furnished with painted steamer chairs, rugs and blooming plants in pottery jars. At the back, rather removed from the main part of the house, were the kitchen, servants' quarters and an open-air laundry. We were really very practical and modern and comfortable. Our kitchen provided for an admirable compromise between old and new methods. It had an English gas-range and a Chinese one. But the proper Chinese atmosphere was preserved by three well-trained servants who called themselves Ah Ching, Ah Ling and Ah Poh. Most Shanghai servants are called simply "Boy" or "Amah" or "Coolie" but ours chose those names, as distinctive for servants there as James and Bridget are with us. Ah Ching did most of the house-work and the running of errands; Ah Ling did the marketing and cooking, giving us a pleasantly varied succession of Chinese and foreign dishes; Ah Poh, the *amah*, looked after Wilfred and attended to my personal wants.

From the first I was fond of Ah Poh, with her finely formed, intelligent features, her soft voice and gentle, unhurried manner. She had served an American mistress before coming to me, but showed a surprising willingness to adopt my particular way of doing things, whether in making beds, in keeping my clothes in order or in entertaining Wilfred. On the other hand, Ah Ching, elderly, grave and full of responsibility, was very partial to his accustomed way of arranging furniture and of washing windows and floors. If left to himself, he would dust odd nooks and corners faithfully, but if I made any formal inspection of his labors, he would invariably slight them—to intimate that I should not be suspicious, as a friend explained—a form of logic that I found highly amusing. Ah Ling, aside from his culinary ability, was chiefly interesting because his eyes were really oblique—as Chinese eyes are supposed to be, and usually are not, and because his hair really curled—as Chinese hair is supposed never to do, and does, occasionally.

For a young pair bent on thrift, we may have seemed very extravagant indeed. In similar circumstances in America, I should probably have thought it extravagant to have even one servant. But this household was a very small one for China and, on our modest income, we maintained it with a satisfactory margin.

Chan-King was helpful and showed great tact and understanding in getting our establishment under way. I would not confess to my utter bewilderment in trying to manage servants who did not understand half of what I said to them. I think he became aware that I was holding on rather hard at times during those first months, and he never failed me. In turn, I helped him revise his papers in the evenings and assisted him with his letters, and he used to call me his secretary. We discovered during that first year in China that we had formed a true partnership.

Our social life was very pleasant. We entertained a great deal, in a simple way. We belonged to a club or two and kept in close touch with the work of the returned students, who have become an important factor in the national life. Though wishing to conserve what is best in the civilization of China, they are bringing western ideas to bear upon the solution of political, sociological and economic problems. Many of these students, as well as other interesting people, both Chinese and foreign, gathered at our house for dinners and teas.

There was a veteran of the customs service, a portly gentleman with bristling white mustache, who had been one of the first group of government students sent to America fifty years before. He told interesting stories of the trials and joys of those early days and humorously lamented the fact that real apple pie was not to be obtained in China. There was a distinguished editor of English publications, a tall, spare figure, whose very quietness suggested reserves of mental power. With him often was a short, energetic man in early maturity—a far-sighted educator and convincing orator. I remember a lively discussion opened up by these two concerning the need for a Chinese magazine devoted to the interests of the modern woman of China—an early dream, which is now being fulfilled. There was a retired member of Parliament with an unfailing zeal for political discussion, who has since returned to the service of his government. Also a smiling young man, who went about persuading Old China of her need for progress, but who could on occasion put aside his dignity to indulge a talent for diverting bits of comedy. There was the Chinese-American son of a former diplomat, who—born in America and coming to China as a grown man—seemed definitely to recognize his kinship with the land of his fathers, a fact that Chan-King and I found interesting for its possible bearing on the future of our own sons. Naturally, most of our friends were the younger modern folk, who were loosening the ancient bonds of formality in their daily lives. But many of the older and more conservative people also used to come to our evening gatherings, where my husband and I received side by side.

As I came to know the Chinese, I was delighted with their social deftness. They stress grace of manner and courtesy as the foundations of all social life. I was pleasantly impressed by the measure of deference that they showed to wives, daughters, sisters and friends—so different from the contempt that western imagination supposes to be their invariable share. Occasionally I noticed a husband carefully translating that his wife might fully enjoy the conversation. Many of the women, however, spoke English excellently. All our receptions and dinners were delightfully free and full of good talk. The Chinese have so beautifully the gift of saying profound things lightly; they can think deeply without being heavy and pedantic.

I remember the first dinner party I attended in Shanghai. It was rather a grand affair, with many guests, all Chinese save me—"and I'm almost Chinese," I said to my husband. The men and women all sat together around one great table, in excellent humor with each other, and the talk was very gay.

A little Chinese woman whom I knew rather well said to me later, "And think of it—only last year in this house we should have been at separate tables!" When I asked her to explain, she said that once men did not bring their guests to their homes at all. Then they brought them, but entertained them in the men's side of the house. Later they admitted women to dine in the same room, but at separate tables, and now, here we are, chatting and dining together quite in western fashion. "I like this much better," the little lady decided.

I was glad to see that all of them wore Chinese dress, for it is most impressively beautiful. I wore my first jacket and plaited skirt that night, a combination of pale green and black satin, and now and then I would see Chan-King's eyes turned upon me with the look I best loved to see there—a clear, warm affection shining in them, a certain steady glow of expression that had love and friendship and understanding in it. I think the sight of me in the dress of his country confirmed in his mind my declaration that I loved China—that I wanted to be a real Chinese wife.

After this, though for certain occasions the American fashion seemed more appropriate, I wore Chinese dress a great deal. I remember a day when Dr. Wu Ting-fang came to dinner, and, as he bowed to me, obviously took note of my garb.

He looked at me very keenly for a moment, as if he meant to ask a serious question. Then he said, in his abrupt manner, "You are happy in that dress?"

"Indeed I am," I answered.

"You like it better than you like American clothes?" he persisted.

I nodded firmly, smiling and catching my husband's eye.

"Then wear it always," said the Doctor, with a pontifical lifting of his fingers.

Oddly enough, my husband did not care for the native feminine fashion of trousers and never permitted me to wear them. I considered them very graceful and comfortable, but gladly adopted the severely plain skirts with the plaits at the sides.

I had put on China, to wear it always, in my heart and mind, and thought only of my husband, his work and his people. In the beginning, I should have been perfectly content to remain cloistered, to meet no one save a few women friends, to go nowhere. Life flowed by me so evenly that I was happy to drift with it, filled with dreams. The noise of hurrying, half-modernized Shanghai reached me but vaguely, deep within my cool, quiet house where the floors were spread with white matting and the walls were hung with symbolic panels. The click of the ponies' feet on the pavement, the thud of the rickshaw coolies' heels as they drew their noiseless, rubber-tired vehicles, the strident scream of the automobile horns, the strange, long cries of the street vendors, all came to me muffled as through many curtains that sheltered me from the world. But my husband insisted that I go about with him everywhere that he felt we should go, that I help him entertain, that I meet and mingle with many people, both foreign and Chinese.

He was always ready to advise me on social matters, a more difficult undertaking than might be supposed. I have already spoken of the many gradations in the meeting of East and West. These alone are confusing enough, and there are further complexities due to the fact that in the two civilizations the fine points of etiquette are often entirely at variance. A single example will suffice—the custom of serving a guest, as soon as seated, with some form of refreshment. In the very conservative Chinese household, if the visitor even touches the cup of tea, placed beside him on a small table, he is guilty of a gross breach of good manners. In the ultra modern household, he must drink the iced summer beverage or the piping hot winter drink, to avoid giving offense. Then there are the variously modified establishments, where he attempts an exact degree of compromise, whether acknowledging the offering merely by a gracious bow, or going further by raising it to the lips for a dainty sip, or being still more liberal and consuming one-half the proffered amount. That such situations are often baffling, even to Young China, I have heard it laughingly confessed in many lively discussions. But though occasional errors are inevitable, sincere good will is truly valued and seldom misunderstood. Chan-King's ability to consider all points of view at once was very helpful to me.

But he forgot to warn me that in Shanghai social calling is proper at any hour of the day from nine o'clock in the morning until ten o'clock at night. I was therefore three days in learning, during a short absence of his, that early morning and late evening calling was an institution, and not an accidental occurrence, as I at first supposed. Finally, Ah Ching gave me a hint. I was in a negligee, preparing for a morning of lazy play with Wilfred and hoping there would be no interruptions, when Ah Ching appeared and announced callers. My face must have expressed surprise and a shade of annoyance, as it had for three days previously at these summonses, for Ah Ching hesitated a moment and then vouchsafed what he plainly considered a valuable piece of information. "In Shanghai," said Ah Ching, "he all time go to see—all time come to see." He paused. "*All* time!" he added firmly and departed. I found this to be literally true and I therefore formed my habits of dress on the assumption that callers demanding the utmost formality of behavior and appearance might be announced at any moment.

Needless to say, Ah Ching's "he" was a pidgin English for "she," for my personal visitors were all women. They were of many nationalities—Chinese, of course, and also American, Canadian, English, Scotch and French. With the Chinese women, especially, I found myself in perfect harmony. Nowhere, I believe, does sincerity and good-will meet with a warmer response. They accepted me with a cordiality that was very real and rendered invaluable assistance in my initiation into the new life. They took me calling, shopping and marketing until Shanghai ceased to be a bewildering maze of crowded thoroughfares; they helped me to understand the complexities of Chinese currency; they explained the intricate points of fashion in dress and recommended skillful tailors.

From the first we were deeply interested in the meeting and blending of East and West that went on about us everywhere, in every field of endeavor. We found unique opportunity for fresh impressions in the Second Far Eastern Olympics held at Shanghai that spring. In the presence of many thousand spectators, China, the Philippines and Japan strove for supremacy in athletic prowess. The affair was managed entirely by Chinese, and during most of the contests my husband was busy on the grounds in official capacity. I sat in the grand-stand with Chinese woman friends, some of whom were returned students, and the rousing cheers, the whole-hearted enthusiasm, brought to us vivid memories of college days in America. The evenings were filled with receptions and garden parties in honor of the visitors. Of course our pleasure in the whole affair was immeasurably heightened by China's well-earned triumph.

As the months passed, Chan-King's high-hearted enthusiasm, his dauntless will to carry through great work in the education of Young China, flagged to some degree, from terrible disillusionment.

This is the problem all returned students have sooner or later to face and conquer. They come home brimming with hope and filled with aspirations toward their country's betterment. And gradually they are forced to acknowledge one enormous fact—that China has been her glorious, grim old self for too many centuries, her feet are sunk too deeply in the earth of her ancient traditions, to be uprooted by one generation of youth—or two or three or a hundred.

Chan-King chafed and worried and worked too hard.[2] Strangely enough, he grew homesick for America, though I did not.

"America strides like a young boy, and China creeps like an old woman!" he said bitterly one day after attending a meeting of the college board, where his modern ideas of education had suffered a defeat at the hands of the reactionary body.

"But China is a wise, wise old woman!" I replied gently.

And very often during this time I would uphold the traditions of the East while Chan-King championed the ways of the western world.

My husband underwent disappointments, irritations and trials that would have been unendurable in a less securely poised nature. As it was, he suffered so in the great things that he had but little patience for the small ones, and I often found him sudden of temper, with a quick asperity of tone and finality of judgment that showed me clearly how great a strain he was under.

But with us there was always love. And Chan-King was very careful to make me understand, even in the midst of small disappointments and vexations, that these things were the universal human annoyances that had nothing to do with regrets or a sense of alienation. I broke into tears one day when a sharp little scene occurred over nothing at all. "O Margaret, my dearest!" he said, taking me in his arms, "these moods mean nothing between us, when we love each other so! Don't take them seriously! What could destroy our happiness now?" In spite of the world-wide difference in our race and upbringing, whatever difficulties of temperamental adaptation we had to meet were merely such as must be faced by any husband and wife in any land.

Yet Chan-King's personal fascination for me, his never-failing appeal to my imagination, was definitely founded on the oriental quality in him: I found throughout the years, in every phase of our relation, a constant, irresistible, always recurring thrill in the idea that we were not of the same race or civilization.

Once when I confessed this fact to him, he said, "Do you love me only because I am Chinese?"

"No—I think I should have loved you no matter what race you came of. But how can I know?"

"I like to feel that you love the essential *me*."

"Yes, but the essential *you* is Chinese."

He thought a moment, "Chinese, yes, but a most respectable member of the Dutch Reformed Church of America!"

"I won't let that injure you in my eyes!" I assured him, laughing. I was of the Anglican faith, and we often referred to the strange mixture of nationalities in our creeds.

My husband, in spite of his firm faith, was not of a deeply religious mind, and of the two I was much more mystical in my beliefs. Love, divine and human, had come to mean everything to me, in a literal and spiritual sense. I believed, obscurely at first, but with increasing surety and faith as time went on, that human love also was not of time only, but of eternity as well. And when I found that Chan-King did not share this belief, I felt, for the only time in all my marriage, alien to him, shut out by an impalpable·veil from his profoundest inner life, which I wished passionately to share in everything. The discovery came hand in hand with our first shadow—only the shadow of a shadow, I might call it, so vague, at the beginning, that we could not feel more than an uneasiness.

Chan-King fell ill, though not seriously, and he recovered quickly.[3] But on the up-curve of returning health he never quite regained the old plane of physical well-being. Signs—oh, the very smallest of signs—warned us of a grave, slow breaking down of his system under phthisis.[4] We could not quite believe it.

His physician advised him to ease the strain of work as much as he could.[5] We talked together in the early hours of many nights, Chan-King always insisting that his depression was the result of temporary fatigue, sure to pass away with a few weeks' repose in the open air of the hills.

It was during this time that I spoke to him of the everlastingness of love and my faith in a life farther on. "Where could death take one of us that the other could not follow?" I asked him, in strange triumph.

His eyes held mine a long minute. His face was very sad. "I am not sure of that. I have no idea of what we shall be to one another in another life. I am only sure that we are all things to each other now."

An inexpressible sense of fear took hold of me. Chan-King seemed at once terribly alien and removed; I could not speak, for I had the feeling of calling in a strange language across a great chasm. I said nothing for fear of distressing him, but he must have sensed my disquietude, for he took my hands and held them to his face and let his eyes shine upon me. "Don't look like that," he said. "We have much time yet to think of eternity." But from the day of this illness the shadow was never once removed from me.

Now we were lured by the residential charms of the French Concession, with its broad, tree-lined avenues and fresh, wind-swept spaces. So we took a new house in a terrace fronting on Avenue Joffre. We liked our large rooms, each with its tiled fireplace, its polished floors laid with Tientsin rugs, its electric lights. There was a grassy lawn with Chinese orchids and a border of palms and magnolias, and just around the corner from us was a public garden where, to Wilfred's delight, dozens of children played each day under the care of their respective *amahs*. Our staff of servants was now increased to five by the addition of a rickshaw coolie and a second *amah*.

Chan-King received shortly after this a letter from his father, the first communication he had had from his family since our marriage. It contained an invitation to return home for a visit, since his mother wished very deeply to see him again.

"I can interpret this in only one way, Margaret," he said in a puzzled tone. "It is an offer of reconciliation. That means that they do not know you are with me."

"Go and see for yourself what it is," I told him. For I would have consented, for his sake, to a reconciliation on almost any terms. I had seen enough of Chinese family life to understand the powerful bonds of affection and interest that bind the clan together, and I felt in my own heart the cruelty of breaking those between mother and son and brother and brother.

"I want to tell them about you," Chan-King answered. "This is my opportunity."

Before accepting their invitation, Chan-King wrote and told them that his wife was with him. And their replies to this proved him right in his first surmise. His family knew he had returned to China and, having heard nothing further of his marriage, had supposed that it was all over. This was not exactly a surprising conclusion for them to reach. More than one foreign woman has refused to accompany her Chinese husband home. I myself came in contact with an occasional half-household, in which a Chinese was held in China by his business affairs while his wife waited for him on the other side of the world. Sometimes, too, she did not wait, and the marriage ended in the conventional way—that is, in the divorce court. Chan-King's people imagined that something of the sort had occurred to him, and were quite ready to wipe out old scores and resume the ties of relationship.

After having written the initial letter of reconciliation, they held to their attitude in a thoroughbred way, only amending their welcome a trifle by requesting him to visit them alone. Very tactfully and gently they put it like this: his father was growing old and any sudden change disturbed him; the household had lately been added to by marriage and births, and he would find everything very much more comfortable if he should come alone.

He went, firmly resolved to change the mind of his family toward me. And I, too, was anxious for them to know that a foreign marriage had not harmed Chan-King. During the six weeks of his absence his letters were cheerfully noncommittal, though he spoke of his happiness in being in his mother's house again. I thought a great deal about that house, the intricate lives of the

people in it and their many degrees of kinship and authority. Chan-King had
told me enough to give me a fairly clear picture of them. I had always admired
their ability to sustain difficult relations under the same roof with the utmost
good temper and mutual courtesy.

Yet I was western enough to feel that Chan-King and I knew each other
better and had been more free to learn each other thoroughly, alone in our
own household, which was growing in quite a Chinese fashion. I expected my
second child and looked forward, with much hope, to the new life, for I had
always been deeply maternal and wanted several children. But to Chan-King
and me our love for each other was the greatly important thing in life—the
reason for all the rest of our existence. We accepted the fact of birth as naturally as we did the change of seasons. Children were an essential to our happiness, but not the dominant essential. We ordered our home for ourselves, as
two lovers who had elected to pass their life together.

Chan-King expressed our views thus: "The Chinese idea is that the family is
the end, the children the means of keeping it up. In the West, the children are
the end, and the home merely the means of keeping them up. You and I have it
perfectly adjusted, I think—the home is for all of us, and all of us have proper
places in it."

Chan-King returned early one morning, and I knew, from my first glimpse
of his face, that his visit had been a fruitful one. I flew to his arms, and, as he
kissed me, I saw that his eyes were serene and contented.

"How is your august mother, my lord?" I asked him with a bow.

"My mother[6] is in good health and wishes to meet her daughter-in-law," he
answered, and, in spite of the bantering tone, I knew he was in earnest.

I wanted to know how this change of feeling had come about.

"When I told them of you," said Chan-King, "my mother was visibly amazed.
'I did not understand!' she kept repeating. 'I did not understand!' and before I
left, she said to me, 'If she is all you tell me she is, why do you not bring her
here?' I didn't mention the fact that this is our first invitation, Margaret! Should
you like to go, my dearest?"

I hesitated a moment. "Yes, but not yet," I answered.

"We will not go for a while," Chan-King assured me.

We talked a great deal about my husband's visit, and I gained new light on
the actual facts of his estrangement from his family and the enormous signifi-
cance that his marriage assumed in the minds of his Chinese relatives.

I can hardly exaggerate the importance of the position held by the eldest
son in the higher class Chinese household. After his father, he is the male head
of the family. His wife is the attendant shadow, the never-failing companion of

his mother. Our phrase, "A man marries," is expressed in Chinese as "He leads in a new woman." Under the old régime he literally did so, for he invariably brought his bride to his ancestral home. The phrase for the marriage of a girl is, "She goes forth from the family." "A new woman" is the term for a bride. The western education of many young men of the Chinese upper class has resulted in some acute readjustment in the ancestral households. Often these elder sons return, marry according to the old custom and live in their parental homes. But often, too, they marry advanced Chinese women, set up establishments and professions of their own, far from their native cities, and live after semi-foreign ways.

In this respect, our case was somewhat typical. As I have already related, Chan-King's mother had been looking forward for years to the marriage of her eldest son with the little Miss Li-Ying. She had expected in her middle age the usual release of the Chinese woman from the bonds of youth. Having been a faithful and obedient wife and daughter-in-law, she rightfully expected to assume authority over her family, leaning on the arm of her son's wife. This younger woman would take her place in the long chain of dutiful daughters; she would help to welcome guests; she would keep up the family shrines; she would perform all manner of household duties under the supervision of her mother-in-law. On the death of her husband's mother, she would become the woman head of the family, responsible for everything, her privileges and authority growing with her years, especially if she were the mother of sons. Her great mission would be to furnish children to the clan, in order that the ancestral shrines might never be without worshippers. I explain these matters at this point in order that I may not be mistaken for a moment when I tell the incident that follows. By this time, I had lived long enough in China to be almost thoroughly orientalized, in so far as my sympathies were concerned, at least, and yet, when Chan-King, after talking for a while about the events of his visit home, came to a full pause and said uncertainly, "There is one thing I wish to tell you, but I am not sure you will understand," I was a trifle apprehensive.

But I answered at once: "Of course I shall understand. China has been kind to me. What have I to fear?"

Chan-King then went on deliberately: "Not until I saw my mother again did I understand that I had done a really cruel thing to her, in depriving her of a daughter-in-law on whom she could lean in her old age. Oh, Margaret, woman's lot is not easy, with all the complexities of parents and brothers and children! And I would have atoned for my share in all this if I could—but of course there was nothing I could do, nothing at all."

And very calmly he told me that shortly after his arrival at home his mother had conferred with him seriously on her need of a daughter-in-law. In accordance with ancient customs she wished him to take a Chinese secondary wife, who would live in the family home, who would be, in a fashion, proxy for me in the rôle of daughter-in-law. Chan-King's mother offered to arrange this marriage for him and assured him that the secondary wife and her children would be well cared for and treated kindly during his long absences.

I listened incredulously, and the question I could not ask was in my eyes. I knew, of course, that the custom of taking secondary wives was not unusual among wealthy families in China, even where both wives lived under the same roof. But I had given it only the most casual thought. And not once had it occurred to me that the problem would touch my life. Brought suddenly level with it, I suffered a shock at the very foundation of my nature. I could not think, of course, in the moment that followed my husband's recital. I only felt a great roaring tide of pain rising about me, a sense of complete helplessness, such as I have never known before or since. I wonder now at my instant subjective readiness to believe that my husband had conformed to this custom of his country; that he had shaken off his western training at his first renewed contact with the traditional habits of his race.

"Did—you—?" I asked, finally, and stopped.

He came to me instantly, his arms about me. When he saw the distress in my face, he frowned, with an odd, remorseful twist of the brows.

"I wonder that you ask," he said. "How could I come back to you—and to your loyalty and trust—with the shadow of that deception between us? I made it very clear to my mother that I would never have any wife but you. It's you and I together, dear one, and no one else so long as we both shall live."

And his words had the solemn sound of a vow renewed. This high honesty of Chan-King's with me was a rock on which I founded my faith. And his final repudiation of an accepted form among his people represented a genuine sacrifice on his part, so far as his material welfare was concerned. As generously and unhesitatingly as he had made the first one, at our marriage, he laid the second votive offering on the altar of our love. He had, you see, according to the view of his father and mother, hopelessly injured them in his marriage. Above all, he had denied in himself the great racial instinct of the Chinese to obey his parents. If he wished to please them, here was his last opportunity. The taking of a Chinese secondary wife would have been a complete atonement in their eyes. At the same time it would have meant his instant restoration to his rightful place among them—first in their affections and inheritance. The family assistance would have placed him at once in the position toward which, without it, he would probably have to struggle for years.

And later I understood how very easily he might have complied without my needing ever to know of the fact. Indeed, I could have lived in his mother's house with a second wife and never have suspected that she was there in that position, so securely welded and impassive is the clan sense, the reserve and remoteness of the personal relation when the family peace and dignity are to be considered.

Some of these matters I had been aware of since my life in China began, some of them I learned that day in talking with Chan-King and others, as I have said, I discovered gradually afterward. But from that day, certainly our relation subtly shifted and settled and crystallized. We both became forever certain that we could not fail each other in any smallest thing. Into my heart came a warmth of repose, like a steadily burning lamp. We were assured of our love beyond any possibility of doubt, ever again. And for a time we experienced a renascence of youthful happiness, a fine fervor of renewed hopes and ambitions, as though spring had come again miraculously, when we had expected October.

The family letters came now regularly to Chan-King, with always a kindly message for me. Evidently relations were to be resumed on the plane of a good friendship, nothing more. But that was so much more than we had dared to hope for that we were perfectly happy to have it so.

Chan-King must have mentioned his slowly failing health, for his mother sent a worried letter to him and asked him to come home for a while once more. Chan-King decided that his affairs would not warrant his absence and wrote her to that effect.

One morning as I sat on the sun-porch, sewing, Ah Ching appeared suddenly before me.

"Master's mother, he downstairs," he announced calmly. I gazed at him without understanding.

"What do you say?"

Ah Ching came nearer. He held up one hand and counted his words off on his fingers slowly. "Missee-sabe-master-have-got-one mother?" he inquired patiently.

"Yes, yes!"

"Well, he just now have come. He downstairs!"

I got to my feet. I was more frightened and nervous than I had ever been. I remembered to be grateful. I was wearing complete Chinese dress—a black skirt and blue velvet jacket. This fact assumed an amusing importance in my mind as I stood there, struggling to get myself in hand. I had planned this meeting a thousand times, and now that it was fairly upon me, I was totally without resource. I progressed downstairs confusedly, running a few swift steps and then stopping short and beginning again slowly. If Chan-King had been there, I should have fled to him and left the entire situation in his hands; but I was alone and certain of one thing only—I meant to win the love of my Chinese mother if I could. Subjectively, all the tales I had heard of Chinese mothers-in-law must have impressed me more than I had admitted, for I remembered something Chan-King had told me long before: "I cannot describe to you the importance of the mother in the Chinese household. She is a complete autocrat, with almost final authority over her sons, daughters-in-law, servants, relatives, everybody except her husband, who is usually absent on his business. Her old age is a complete reversal of the restraint and discipline of her youth."

I stopped short at the door of the drawing-room. I saw my husband's mother for the first time. She had become to me a personality of almost legendary grandeur, and I felt a little wave of surprise go over me that she looked somehow so real and alive and genuine. She sat in a big, tall-backed chair, her hands spread flat on her knees. Her face was the face of the young mother in the photograph Chan-King had shown me, only grown older and a trifle more severe. She was dressed in black brocade, its stiff folds and precise creases accentuating her dignity. Under the edges of her skirt glimmered her tiny gray shoes, embroidered in red and green. At her side stood the male relative who had accompanied her—a Chinese gentleman of the old school, in a long gown of dark silk. Behind her chair stood a maid and two men-servants.

I knew that she spoke no English, and as yet I had no knowledge of her southern dialect. There was a sharp pause in the dead-silent room while we regarded each other.

I I I
FIRST DAUGHTER-IN-LAW

I clasped my hands in the Chinese way, smiled and bowed. My Chinese mother[1] rose at once and took a step toward me, balancing on her tiny feet with the aid of a thick, gold-headed cane. I saw that she was unusually tall. Then, surprisingly, she extended her hand, American fashion, and I shook it, the eyes of each of us still searching the other's face. I saw in hers the look I needed for reassurance—the mingled kindness and apprehension—a trace of the anxiety that I am sure was the very counterpart of my own expression. I knew then that her heart was no more certain than mine was, and that this meeting was as important to her as it was to me.

Ah Ching brought forward my chair and we sat down together, smiling at each other, letting our gestures speak for us. Finally she stretched forth her right hand, palm down, measuring the height of a small child from the floor, inclining her head toward me, her eyebrows up in a question. I made a pillow of my two hands, laid my head upon it, eyes closed, and then pointed up. We were both delighted at this simple pantomime. The elderly man—her cousin—looked pleased in sympathy and even the three solemn servants smiled a little. She asked me in gestures where my husband was. I waved widely and comprehensively toward the street, in the general direction of the city. She nodded, settling back a trifle, drawing a long breath. We had reached the end of our power to converse without the aid of an interpreter.

When I heard Chan-King's ring at the gate, I hurried out to meet him with the news. He was even more excited than I was and hastened ahead of me to the house. I walked very slowly in order that they might have their first greeting undisturbed, and, when I arrived, they were beaming upon each other and talking the South Province dialect over a very sleepy and cherubic infant, whom Chan-King, with paternal pride, had ordered down to greet his grandmother at once.

The retinue settled, Chan-King informed me that our mother would remain with us for six weeks. During this time, I learned the art of pantomime beyond anything I had ever hoped for in one of my undemonstrative nature. My Chinese mother and I conversed with eyebrows, hands, smiles, noddings and shakings of the head, much turning of the eyes. I had an instant affection and admiration for her, and she adopted toward me a gently confidential attitude that pleased me very much.

She had brought presents for us, in the Chinese way: for me, a delicately wrought chain of Chinese gold in a box of carved sandalwood; for Wilfred, a dozen suits of Chinese clothes in the bright patterns worn by children of the Orient, and so becoming to the proud, wee man that, arrayed in them, he seemed already to be coming into his heritage. She also brought great hampers of fresh fruits—pomeloes, lichees and dragon's-eyes—and countless jars of preserved fish and meats and vegetables, which had been Chan-King's favorites when he was a boy at home.

Madame Liang had the Chinese woman's love for shopping. Accompanied by her cousin and the servants, we went from silk merchant to porcelain dealer, and from brass worker to rug weaver, gathering treasures. Though she carried on most of her negotiations through her cousin, she bargained with a firmness and a sense of values that I admired very much. In the silk shops she bought marvelous brocaded satins and embroidered silks and she had me select the pattern I wanted for myself. Though she preserved most carefully the distinctive features of the dress of her own province, she was much interested in Shanghai styles and examined my wardrobe critically, noting the short sleeves with tight-fitting undersleeves and the skirts with seven plaits—not five, as in Canton, for example—at each side.

Notwithstanding the popular western fancy that fashions never change in China the Chinese woman is painstakingly particular as to the exact length and fullness—or scantiness—of her coats, skirts and trousers. She is carefully precise about the width of bias bands or braid or lace that she uses for trimming, the number and arrangement of fastenings, the shape and height of her collar. All of these details vary as tyrannically from season to season—under Shanghai guidance—as certain style features do with us under the leadership of New York or Paris. Moreover, as against our four seasons, the fashion devotee of China takes account of eight, each with its appropriate style and weight of clothing.

At home Mother sewed a great deal, using her hands gracefully and very competently in spite of the long curved finger-nails on her left hand. My American sewing-machine fascinated her. She had an excellent hand-power machine at home, Chan-King explained, but mine worked with a treadle and she wished to try it. I took the tiny, brightly shod feet in my hands and set one forward and one backward on the iron trellis. And she moved them very well, alternately, and ran several seams with energy.

Chan-King, his mother and I went to Chinese cafés together and Madame Liang was pleased and amused to see that I not only used chopsticks with ease but had a real taste for Chinese food. We used to treat ourselves to all sorts of epicurean dishes: spiced chicken and duck, shark's fins, bird's-nest soup with pigeon eggs (my favorite delicacy), seaweed and bamboo shoots, candied persimmons, lotus-seeds and millet pudding with almond tea.

Once, in a roof-garden café, where I was wearing American clothes, my use of chopsticks aroused considerable interest among neighboring groups of diners, and stray comments reached us, for the Chinese are always pleased to see foreigners familiar with their customs. "No doubt she is a missionary lady," a young woman remarked in my husband's native dialect. Hearing and understanding, Mother immediately said, in clear, gracious tones, "My son, perhaps your wife would like to have some American food now." Chan-King translated for me both comment and suggestion, and I felt pleased to learn that, at any rate, my Chinese mother was not ashamed, in a public place, to acknowledge her American daughter.

Mother was fond of the drama and, since Shanghai had some excellent theaters, we made up several parties during her stay.

The great semicircular stage, on which a famous old historical play that we saw was acted, was hung with gorgeous embroideries, laid with a thick Peking rug of immense size and brilliantly lighted by electricity—as was the entire theater. The actors wore the magnificent official and military robes of an early dynasty. As on the Elizabethan stage, women's parts were taken by men, who achieved by cleverly constructed shoes the effect of bound feet. I found the deafening drums and gongs a little trying, at moments, and the crude property make-shifts somewhat incongruous with the wonderfully elaborate hangings and costumes. But, being familiar with the story, I understood the action and so evidently enjoyed it that Mother was surprised anew, as Chan-King afterward told me. We sat in our balcony box, above the vague tiers of lower seats packed with a restless audience of men, women and many children in the arms of their *amahs*. On the wide front rail of our box was the inevitable pot of tea, with room also for such fruits, sugar-cane, melon-seeds, or meat-and-rice dishes as we wished to purchase from the endless variety offered by eager boys in round caps and blue cotton gowns. Now and then an attendant came with a huge teakettle to refill our teapot, and once he offered us the usual steaming hot towels for sticky fingers. Chan-King waved these away energetically. "Awful custom," he said to me. "Unhygienic. How can they do it?" And he added something of the kind to his mother in Chinese. She regarded him with comprehension, a tiny gleam of superior wisdom in her eyes. But she made no reply.

She had taken a fancy to Wilfred, who by this time had a fair vocabulary of Chinese, which he always used in talking to his *amah*. He was a handsome child, typically Chinese, very charming in his manner, very fond of his *amah* and his indulgent grandmother. Madame Liang would take his chin in her hands and study his features intently, nodding her head with approval. Then she would stroke his round black poll and give him melon-seeds or almonds from her pocket. Wilfred used a weird mixture of dialects—a confusion of Mandarin and the Shanghai vernacular, with a dash of Cantonese from his *amah*. Madame Liang set out patiently to teach him her own dialect as well.

When her visit was ended, our mother said to Chan-King, "This is a Chinese house, with a Chinese wife in it. Everything is Chinese. I could never have believed it without seeing, for I thought your wife was a western woman. I am happy." And she told him again that we must come and visit with her, for she needed us.

Chan-King's father, a member of an old, established firm in the import and export trade in the Philippines, was away, looking after his business or exchanging visits with friends of his own age and rank. His home-comings were in the nature of a vacation. The management of the household depended on Madame Liang.

As she talked, I realized by her face, by Chan-King's answers, by all that I knew of Chinese family life, that we were a part of that clan and should be so always. A hint of the solidarity I now feel with my husband's family came to me. We were not separate from them; nor should we be.

After our mother was gone, Chan-King said something of this sort to me, quoting what she had said about my not being western. "But I love you to be western in this sense," he told me, "that you and I have companionship and freedom and equality in our love. That is what makes me happiest."

Before Chan-King and I closed the house in Shanghai to depart for the southern hills, our second son, Alfred, was born.[2] An American woman asked me, when he was about six weeks old, if I did not feel a sense of alienation at the sight of the wee, oriental face at my breast. Quite simply and truthfully I answered, no. My husband was not in any way alien to me. How then, could our child be so?

His coming provided me with a welcome excuse to remain at home quietly for a short while. I now attempted to learn, at the same time, both Mandarin and the dialect of Chan-King's province—a method of study that hampered me constantly at first. But my husband was an encouraging teacher, and I began uncertainly to use my new knowledge, trying it mostly on my young son Wilfred, who was the real linguist of the family. He took my Chinese very seriously. I cannot say so much for Chan-King, who was greatly amused at my inflection.

Toward the close of the year, I decided to take a place as teacher of English and history in a Chinese girls' high school.[3] Chan-King was surprised when I told him that I wished to teach but he offered no objection, and watched with interest my progress through the year. I loved my teaching. Still more I loved the girls in my classes. Collectively and individually I found them supremely worth while in spirit and mind. I cannot say how lovely the young womanhood of China seemed to me. I began to yearn for a daughter, and when, toward the close of the second term, I found that I might, perhaps, have my heart's desire, I realized that my husband shared it.

In the early fall, our mother wrote and asked us to come south for the cold season. She also expressed the hope that the coming grandchild might be born in her own province. Chan-King had been encouragingly strong for over a year, but he had always found the northern winters hard. We decided that the time had come to fulfil our promise of visiting the ancestral home. Chan-King secured six months' leave of absence.

Within ten days we had closed our affairs temporarily, dismissed the servants, with the exception of the *amah* and the faithful Ah Ching, got our boxes together and bidden our friends farewell. The leaves were falling on the avenue; the plants were shriveled at the edges on the sun porch; the winds blew ominously shrill under the eaves. Chan-King grew pale and began to cough again. Out of the teeth of the terrible Shanghai winter we fled into the hospitable softness of the South.

By a large steamship we started out on what was ordinarily a brief journey. But by those war-time schedules, changes and delays were the invariable rule. After three unforeseen changes and as many delays we reached a port just over the line in my husband's province. There we stopped, intending to go on three days later by the little, battered, tramp steamer that puffed noisily at the dock, putting off dried fruits and dyes, taking on rice and cloth and sandalwood. But we did not go on, as it happened. Instead, a tiny, smiling, competent woman physician, wearing the southern costume and possessed of a curious fund of practical wisdom in medical matters, attended me in her native hospital at the birth of our daughter Alicia.[4]

On a vaguely gray, gently stimulating winter morning, ten days later, our bouncing little ship—for I had cajoled Chan-King into allowing me to travel—stood to, out from port, and sampans came to meet us. Like giant fish, bobbing and dipping and swaying upon the waves, these sampans with their great eyes painted on each side of the prow and their curious, up-curved sterns, came toward us in a gala-fleet, rowed by lean, over-muscled men in faded blue cotton garments. I was very gay and much exhilarated by the soft sunshine that broke through the mist as I climbed down with Chan-King's help into one of these boats.

The harbor was busy with small craft—flat-bottomed gigs or baggage-boats besides the junks, whose square brown sails swung creaking in the wind. Two Chinese men-of-war rose over us, their vast, bulky sides painted battle-ship gray.

Out and beyond, an island not more than a mild long turned its irregular profile toward us, a long mass of huge gray boulders jutting abruptly from a sparkling sea. As we were being rowed in to the mainland, we were near enough to the island to see quite plainly the tile-roofed houses surrounded by arched verandas, repeated again and again in long, undulating lines that gave a pleasantly lacy effect. The island was shaded with trees in winter foliage, not the brilliant green of summer, but the sage-green and pale tan of November. Through this intermittent curtain the walls of the houses shone in dull blue and coral pink and clear gray. Jagged cacti shot up among the bulbous rocks and everywhere the scarlet poinsettia set the hills aglow with patches of brilliant color. I loved this island instantly. I said to Chan-King, "This is our Island of the Blest, where we shall live when we are old."

At the jetty, Ah Ching went up to hail sedan-chair bearers, and soon I was borne rapidly along a few yards ahead of my husband's chair.

I was filled with a delicious elation at being in Chan-King's province, so near to the very village that he knew as a little boy. With enormous curiosity, I peeped through the curtain-flaps, which were transparent from within. We were passing through the town that lay along the water's edge—a bright, open little place, where the small houses, with curved tiled roofs, hugged the ground. We went through the crooked streets, which were really nothing more than broad paths, at a steady pace. We left the ragged edges of the town and began to ascend the hills. I raised my curtains a trifle and ventured to look out freely. Emotion surged up in me. I wished to cry for joy in this home-coming, for it was our real home-coming together, and I felt a secret share in all the life my husband had known here.

Up the narrow, twisting path we wound, toward the hills, which were cov-

ered with a smoky, amber mist. Scattered closely along the upward road, apart
from the dwellings, were small terraces enclosing plots of cultivated ground,
filled with growing things. Wherever the folk could find a lush, flat place on
the stony hills, robbed by deforestation of all but grass, they had planted their
vegetables. These little patches of color, coaxed by thrifty gardeners out of the
soil washed into the hill-pockets, added a festive, humorous note to the winter
landscape, otherwise so brown and sear. I thought frivolously of a solemn
giant wearing his party nosegays. The hills billowed away immensely, until
they were silhouettes against the dull orange and ashy purple of the morning
sun struggling through the clouds. Solid, steeply curved, narrow bridges of
stone made us a path over the frequent streams that rushed downward to the
valley.

Here we came full upon the ancestral village of my husband's family. It lay,
compact and many-roofed, upon the side of a hill, as intricately woven and
inevitable-looking as a colony of birds' nests, as naturally a part of the earth as
though it had sprung from planted seeds. Rows of walls ran along the main
thoroughfare. There were few people astir yet and the doors were closed in all
the low-eaved plaster and stone houses.

Our chairs were set down before a tall, hooded gate in a wall of stone-gray.
Ah Ching knocked. The gates were opened, and servants came hurrying out,
accompanied by three leaping black Chow-dogs, which barked in frantic chal-
lenge till Chan-King spoke to them and changed their menace into joyous
welcome.

We entered a spacious courtyard and crossed an exquisite garden, one of
the most beautiful I saw in China. An artificial lake rippled placidly, disturbed
only by the darting goldfish. Laurel- and magnolia-trees darkened the paths. A
thicket of bamboo wavered and cast its reflection in the water at the edge of
the lake.

Chan-King helped me from the chair and together we passed into the main
hall through the wide-flung doors. Madame Liang, early apprised of our arrival, was standing there, and my first sight of her gave me a renewed sense of
home-coming. I was dimly aware of a large hall, at the back of which stood a
high altar, with wreaths of sweet-smelling smoke rising in straight columns
before lettered tablets and brilliant images under glass cases. The glitter of
golden and scarlet embroideries against the wall splintered the dimness with
rays of light like sunshine through a prism. Heavily carved blackwood chairs
with tea-tables and also marble-topped stools with gay, brocaded cushions
were ranged about the room.

We passed through this main hall into the apartment of Madame Liang, where I was given a chair, and I sat, suddenly remembering that I was very tired.

Other members of the family, distant relatives and first cousins, and guests, all women, came in and I was presented to them. Madame Springtime, wife of the second son, did first honors for the family. She was so very youthful—only seventeen—and so wistfully other-worldly that among those mature house-wives, clever and practical managers of their households and husbands' es-tates, she seemed like a branch of peach-bloom. In festal garb of jade-green and lavender—embroidered shoes on her tiny feet and an embroidered head-dress crowning her shining black hair and framing the oval of her shy, smiling face, with its sloe-black eyes—she came bearing a lacquered tray and present-ing to each of us sweet tea, in cups of finest porcelain with standards and covers of silver and with tiny silver spoons having flower-shaped bowls.

The pretty little tea ceremony was then repeated by various members of the family, while the small sons were given hot milk and cakes. An eager group gathered about the tiny new daughter, still sleeping peacefully.

A bubbling, busy little lady, about the age of Madame Liang, leaned over me, with a quizzical smile, and bobbed her gay, pretty head emphatically at me when my mother introduced her as Madame Chau. Elaborately dressed in rich colors, in direct contrast to my soberly garbed mother, she was as merry as Madame Liang was grave and she tripped about on her almost invisible "golden lily" feet with an energy that yet did not destroy the grace of her "willow walk."

But the many-colored costumes, the great curtained bed on one side, the voices—all suddenly seemed far away. And, as I wavered, smiling deter-minedly, I heard my husband's voice. "Mother thinks you are tired; so this woman will show you to our room, where you must lie down and rest."

Some time later, as I lay resting—with Alicia sleeping on my arm—on the bed, which had purple curtains and soft white blankets, Chan-King stepped quietly into the room.

"Feel as comfortable as you look?" he asked and, when I nodded drowsily, he touched a box of cakes.

"These were brought to you by Madame Chau, the busy little lady out there. You know—" he hesitated a moment, "she would have been my mother-in-law, if I hadn't insisted on your mother instead!" and he gave my cheek a gentle pinch.

I was now wide-awake. "The little bird-lady out there—mother of Li-Ying?" I asked. "Where is Li-Ying, then?"

"They didn't tell me anything directly," Chan-King answered. "But I gather from several pointed conversations carried on in my hearing that Madame Chau has just returned from her daughter's house in Singapore. Just imagine: little Li-Ying is married, too, and also has three children—two girls and a boy. I think," said my Chinese husband, with charming complacence, putting a hand over mine and stooping to kiss Alicia's pink, sleeping face, "I think our arrangement is much better. Sons should be older; then daughters are properly appreciated!"

At noon, after an hour's quiet sleep, I was again aroused by Chan-King, who stood beside a maid-servant with a tray.

I sat up. "I expected to be out for luncheon," I said, preparing to rise.

Chan-King look perturbed. "Stay where you are," he warned. "My mother has just been scolding me for allowing you to travel with a ten-days-old baby. 'As if I could do anything about it!' I told her, blaming it all on Eve in the most approved Christian fashion! She admires your spirit, but thinks that, for your health's sake, you should rest two weeks longer at least!"

I lay down meekly. "Very well," I said. "Obedience is my watchword!"

And for the prescribed time I lay in my pretty room—all my senses deeply responsive to the life going on in a Chinese household: the clang of small gongs that summoned the servants; much laughter coming in faintly or clearly as my doors were opened or shut; the tap of lily feet along the passageway; the glimmer of Madame Springtime's radiant pink or blue robes as she entered to inquire after my welfare or bring some new delicacy that had been procured for me. The smoke of incense from the altar floating into the room at intervals, with a pungent sweetness that roused vague memories and emotions. Everything in the house—hangings, clothes, furnishings—was saturated with this aroma. Mingled with a bitter smell, which is distilled by immense age, and touched with the irritative quality of dust, this odor now means China to me and it is more precious than all other perfumes in the world.

"But, Chan-King, life is nothing but food!" I protested, about the third day, when my fourth meal had been served to me early in the afternoon.

"But the quantities are small," he answered. "Much better way, don't you think, than taking great meals many hours apart?"

Early in the morning, the young maid assigned to me would bring in a bowl of hot milk and biscuit. In our apartment, at half past eight, she would serve breakfast, consisting of soft-boiled rice—congee—with various kinds of salty, sweet and sour preparations. At eleven o'clock there was turtle soup or chicken broth. At noon came tiffin, which consisted of substantial meat and vegetable dishes, fish and soup, and dry-boiled rice. Our mid-afternoon refreshment was noodles of wheat or bean-flour, or perhaps a variety of fancy cakes. Tea, kept hot by a basket-cozy, was always on hand in every room. At seven the family dined, and, after the two weeks were up, I joined them, sitting at the first table with Mother and my husband. Dinner was an elaborate meal, in courses, with rice at the close. At bedtime came hot milk again, or sweet congee or perhaps tea, brewed from lotus-seed or almonds. I was continually nibbling. I thought Chinese food delicious, particularly in my husband's province, noted for its delicious "crunchy" fried things.

But Chan-King had yearnings for American dishes. I gave the head cook minute instructions for preparing fricasseed chicken, fresh salads, beefsteak with Spanish sauce—even American hot cakes, and he enjoyed the American canned goods, with butter, cheese, jams and bread, which were brought in frequently from the port.

An episode that caused much merriment was Chan-King's initiation of his family into the mystery—and history—of chop suey. The rich joke of that "made-in-America" Chinese dish is penetrating to every household where the returned student is found. In Shanghai we had heard with amusement how the bewildered chef of the Y.M.C.A. café had gone down to one of the great trans-Pacific liners lying in port, to learn from the head cook on board just what this "chop suey," which all his returned student patrons were demanding, might be. Now, with memories of old college club activities prompting us, and with a skillful cook to carry out our directions, Chan-King and I introduced into the ancestral home that most misunderstood dish in all the world. The family agreed that, though vaguely familiar, it was unlike anything they had ever tried before, and they decided without dissenting vote that it was superior to fricasseed chicken, Spanish steak or hot cakes.

At this time, my husband's brother, Lin-King, came home for a brief stay. I decided from photographs that he resembled his father, who was still away. Lin-King and Madame Springtime seemed well-suited to each other and happy, although the marriage had been arranged by their families and they had never seen each other before the ceremony. I decided that the old custom had much merit, after all—for other people—and said so to my husband, adding, "When our children are grown, we must have them all marry Chinese." Chan-King looked at me long in silence and then, sighing, humorously, he asked, "What of their father's example, my dear?"

Since my Chinese was still bookish and unpracticed in the all-important matters of tone and local idiom, I could not converse with the family, and at the dinner-table and in my mother's apartment I was as silent and meek and pleasant of manner as Madame Springtime herself. Madame Springtime served formal tea to our many guests in absolute silence, with a sweet, fixed smile in the corners of her red mouth. I watched her with consuming interest, for she was acting as first daughter-in-law in my stead.

The machinery of life ran with the smoothness of long habit and complete discipline. The meals were served, the apartments kept in exquisite order and the children cared for by a corps of servants trained in minutiae by an exacting mistress, who knew precisely what she wanted. Our days were left free for the practice of small courtesies, the exchange of pretty attentions and the care of the ancestral altar.

From the ceremonies that took place before this altar at various times, my husband kept himself, his wife and children sedulously aloof. It was neither asked nor expected that he would do otherwise, just as our attendance at the little mission church was accepted without question. At other times, however, I had ample opportunity to study the altar and to enjoy the beauty of its massive carvings, its elaborate incense-burners and candlesticks, its exquisitely wrought embroideries. A porcelain image of the Buddhistic Goddess of Mercy in her character of Son-Giver, set within a large glass case, fascinated me by its remarkable resemblance to certain Catholic images. But the ancestral tablets interested me more, and the respect that I have always accorded objects sacred to others was in this instance mingled with profoundly personal feelings: the interblended characteristics of those men and women so many years dead and gone lived on in the man who was my husband; their life currents pulsed warmly in the veins of my children; perhaps some deep insight gained beyond the grave enabled them to know how truly I acknowledged my debt to them, how earnestly I hoped those children might not prove unworthy of their heritage.

With the help of Chan-King's coaching and my personal observations, I soon learned the gracious routine of the house. At ten o'clock every morning I presented myself at the door of Madame Liang's apartment and sat with her for several hours, often over tiffin, even till tea-time, if she signified a desire for my company. If the weather was fair, we would walk in the garden, she leaning lightly on my arm, her cane tapping on the flagstones. At times, also, tea was served here, with the small children joining us for hot milk and sweet cakes.

I was several days in getting the members of the household identified in their proper relations, for there were thirty persons gathered in that big, low-roofed, rambling compound behind the high, enveloping wall. They were nearly all women, and two-thirds of them servants. The quiet, soft-mannered woman relatives spent nearly all of their time in their own apartments.

Madame Liang's powerful personality, silent and compelling, paled the colors of nearly all the temperaments around her. Her friend Madame Chau was immensely comforting to her, for she could not be persuaded to take anything very seriously. Madame Liang laughed with her more than with anyone else. While they busily embroidered, they gossiped, and I listened to their musical speech with its soft southern accents and chiming, many-toned cadences.

I used to think, as I sat in a deep-cushioned chair, nursing the small Alicia, with a pot of tea at my elbow, that Madame Liang, in her gorgeous, heavily carved, black-and-orange bed, enclosed on three sides by panels of painted silk and draped over the front with silk curtains held back by tasseled brocaded bands, was a link in the Chain of Everlasting Things. She had come into the house exactly as "new women" had done century after century, and she had lived out her life unquestioningly according to their precepts and example. There was a monumental, timeless dignity about her as she sewed and talked of simple matters. In her presence, I felt young and facile and terribly unanchored.

I talked these things over with Chan-King in the dark of the night, when all the household was silent. He was interested in my reactions, knowing they were the outcome of a profound personal love for his family and sympathy with everybody in it. Spiritually, Chan-King also was in sympathy with his family. Practically—well, as I have said, there were moments when he longed for American food, and his first deed in the house was to order the bed curtains removed from our apartment.

They were removed, and nothing was said. A wonderful spirit of courtesy and toleration prevailed in the family life, with a complete absence of that criss-cross of personal criticism that our western freedom of speech permits. Not that there were not undercurrents, intimate antagonisms here and there, personal sacrifices and sorrows. But they were not recognized, for in Chinese life individual claims are eternally relinquished in the interest of clan peace and well-being. There was one authority, and it was vested in Madame Liang. Such a system makes for harmony and preserves the institution of the family, on which all China is founded.

Making no conscious effort, I myself yet became so imbued with this spirit that, when the government summons came for Chan-King to report in Peking early in the new year, I choked down my anguish and said, "How splendid for us all, Chan-King! When are you going?"

We were in the last week of the old year, and at Madame Liang's earnest entreaty my husband delayed his departure (as the summons permitted), that, in the midst of his family, he might celebrate the most delightful of all holi-days. Delicious cooking odors now drifted about everywhere, new clothes for everyone were made ready, and faces took on a shining happiness.

One evening after a visit with his mother, Chan-King came to me, laughing heartily. "Mother reminds me," he said, "that for three days it is customary for the maids, when sweeping the floor, to pile the dust carefully in a corner in-stead of throwing it out, lest the family good fortune should be thrown out with it. But she says of course it is only an old superstition and if you like you may tell the maid to remove the sweepings as usual." I laughed, too. Then I said, "Tell Mother we shall do our part toward keeping good fortune in the family." "For three days, also," continued Chan-King, "no harsh or scolding word is to be spoken by anyone. And therefore," he went on sonorously, "your tyrannical Chinese husband will cease to lecture his American wife—who is certain to need it, though." I looked into his eyes, bright with irrepressible gaiety, and suddenly I kissed them shut, my own eyes misty. "Oh, my dearest," I whispered, "you are just a little boy at home again, in spite of the silver threads." And I smoothed the black locks, already sprinkled with gray. "Chan, I love the Chinese New Year!" I said.

Even now I see it all again. My husband was wearing a long, dignified gown of dark green satin—unfigured, as is customary for officials—dark green trou-sers, short brown jacket, lined with soft fur, black satin cap and black boots. Wilfred was quite a young gentleman in long gown of blue-green silk, braid-trimmed jacket of dark green, blue trousers and red-tufted cap. Chubby Alfred was dressed in lavender jacket, scarlet trousers, a tiger-faced apron of red, white and black, embroidered slippers and a gay little knitted cap. Alicia, whom the whole family loved best in her frilled white American dresses, added now a pink silk jacket and an adorable little pink and black cap, which gave an oriental grace to her features. I wore my latest Shanghai creation, in pale lilac-and-black figured satin. Guests came and went incessantly, and we made our calls in the village. The air was filled with odors of spice, molasses, roasted meats, seed-cakes and millet candy with sounds of firecrackers, gongs and happy voices.

But it was over at last. The time for my husband's departure had come.[5]

With silent expertness, Ah Ching set about packing. In three days Chan-King was ready to go. He was coaching me in the household phrases I should need most in making myself understood without his help. Madame Liang de-cided that, during my husband's absence, I should assume my position as first daughter-in-law. I had no apprehension in regard to the minute, exacting duties that would devolve upon me as a right-hand companion to my husband's mother, for I loved her, but I was not sure of my tact or my deftness, and I felt strung up painfully at the thought of my immediate future.

After the hourly companionship of months, parting from Chan-King was very terrible indeed. He was in and out of our apartment, moving about the house with restless energy, arranging final details. At last he came and stood beside me. "Tell me good-by now, dearest," he whispered. "Afterward—out there—we shall have no opportunity." He drew me close and we kissed with deep feeling, the tears in my eyes refusing to be suppressed any longer.

"Don't cry," he begged, with unaccustomed emotion. "Don't cry, or I can't leave you!" Then he held my face up and dried my tears with his handkerchief and said solemnly, "Smile at me!" And I smiled.

We went across to his mother's apartment, and she came out, the tears on her cheeks not staunched. Joined by the rest of the family, we accompanied him to the entrance and then to the gate, which stood open, almost blocked by the waiting sedan-chair. Chan-King was in Chinese dress, and as he stood there—profile toward me—among the group of servants, giving his final directions, he seemed more oriental, more absorbed into his country, than I remembered ever to have seen him.

He made a profound bow to his mother, with formal words of leave-taking, and gave me a grave little nod. Then, without looking back, he stepped into the chair, the curtains were drawn, and the coolies trotted off down the steep path, followed a little way by the bounding black dogs.

Mother and I stood together, after the others had gone, and watched his chair jostling down the narrow, paved way. Then we turned and looked at each other—rueful smiles on our mouths, tears in our eyes. We shook our heads at each other. I half raised a hand to my heart, and let it fall. I think both of us found our lack of mutual language a welcome excuse for silence.

Madame Liang turned toward the house. The gates closed behind us. I gave her my arm in support until we reached the doorway; then I stepped a pace behind her as she entered. Without speaking, I waited until she had knelt at the altar, and the incense was rising in clouds before the imperturbable images under their glass cases. Then I attended her to her own apartment. My life as a real Chinese daughter-in-law had begun.

Mae Franking with her children, Nelson, Alason, and Cecile, circa 1924.

Mae Watkins, circa 1908.

The Watkins family, circa 1902. Mae is next to her mother; her sister, Gwen, is beside their father.

Tiam Hock Franking, circa 1906.

Tiam Hock Franking age eight, with his parents and unidentified girl.

Tiam Hock Franking with Mae and Nelson after his 19 June 1913 graduation from the Detroit College of Law.

I V
THE ETERNAL HILLS

As I followed my Chinese mother into her apartments, I thought of the benevolent croakings of friends. Their words rattled through my memory like pebbles shaken in a pail: "She can never be happy with a Chinese husband!" Later it was, "It is all very well in America, but wait until she goes to China." When I had happily established myself there, "Heaven help her," said they, "if she tries to live with her Chinese mother-in-law!" In Shanghai, foreign friends had predicted, "Oh, yes, she's lovely in *your* house, but wait until you try living in *her* house!"

"This is the last ditch, Margaret," I said to myself. "Take it clear! Either you are about to make one more argument against intermarriage, or you are going to settle the question forever so far as your case is concerned."

Mother and I went to dinner together, somewhat later than usual. We attacked our food very bravely, eyes down. I glanced up inadvertently, and the sight of tears on her cheeks released mine, too. I leaned forward and took her hand and we struggled with a sentence or two. "No tears!" I said. "Be patient!" she answered.

Next morning after the *amah* had dressed young Alicia, while the cheerful child was following me about the room with her eyes and talking merry baby talk, I took her up and went, earlier than usual, to see Mother. I found her sitting up in bed. She was dressed for the day, and the blankets were rolled back against the side of the wall, making a comfortable couch for her. Thinking of Chan-King, I looked at the row of little cabinets extending across the back, halfway up toward the canopy. I remembered Chan-King's telling me of the year when he was still small enough to stand under these fascinatingly carved cabinets, where his mother stored her trinkets and toilet articles, embroidery silks, perfumes and the endless paraphernalia of her quiet life, and of the pride he felt when he bumped his head one day and found that he must stoop to be comfortable.

Wilfred was just high enough now to stand easily under the cabinets, but, in some mysterious fashion, the little image of him presented at this moment to my fancy became that of the small, far-away Chan-King, whom I was forever re-creating in my mind as I went about the house where he had lived his pleasant youth.

This morning I laid Alicia on the bed near Madame Liang. She bent over her and made a *moue* into the rosy face. I was much pleased when Madame Liang was unusually attentive to Alicia, though my sense of justice always reminded me that my own Scotch mother would probably have made more of the boys. But our Alicia was the first daughter in two generations of my husband's family, and, even though the sons were of priceless value to the clan, she was loved and cherished tenderly. It seemed to me at times that the household was more fond of her than of all the boys together, including Madame Springtime's young Kya-Song, who filled the left wing of the compound with his shouts of glee as he played riding-horse on his precarious bamboo stool. I remembered with amusement the western idea that daughters are unwelcome, always, in Chinese families.

While Madame Liang patted the baby, talking to her coaxingly, I asked what she wished me to do.

She indicated on her dressing-table a box of stereoscopic views, which I brought to her. They formed a complete story, but had become very much confused. As I could read the foreign titles, would I kindly arrange the pictures in proper sequence? The ease and speed with which I accomplished this task won her instant approbation.

This was merely one of the numberless small things I did for her thereafter. In my new estate I was in attendance on my mother during many hours of the day. I walked with her in the garden in fine weather, I sat with her and sewed, threading needles as for my own mother and even helping her to make those marvelous small shoes that she fashioned so carefully to the form of her feet. One day I told her how amazed I had been when I first learned from Chan-King that Chinese wives made the family shoes, but how readily I could understand, when I saw the dainty embroidered foot-wear he referred to, that shoemaking was indeed a womanly craft.

She and Madame Chau used to take great pride in making for themselves the most frivolous of shoes. Madame Chau's were the smaller, being barely two and one-half inches long, whereas those of my mother were twice that length and different in shape. I discovered the reason for this: Madame Chau clung tenaciously to the old style; but Mother had gradually let out her bandages and altered their arrangement, keeping pace with the change that followed the abolition of the old custom.

I became deeply interested in the custom of foot-binding. In Shanghai, all the pupils of my school and (with certain notable exceptions) the women of my social world had natural feet, and the majority of them wore American pumps and Oxfords or English boots. Bound feet, though I saw them frequently in public, seemed very remote. But now, save the girls of twelve and under, who had profited by the new order of things, the women among whom I lived all had bound feet. It may be worth noting, when one remembers how America, with its own great unwashed, jokes at the expense of the Chinese of whatever rank or station, that, in accordance with the fastidious cleanliness of upper class Chinese, the bound feet were exquisitely cared for, and the narrow, white, specially woven bandages were changed every two or three days. As I watched the daintily shod women of my mother's household, I realized that never before had I appreciated, in reading the literature of my adopted country, the aptness of comparing the walk of a woman with bound feet to the grace of bamboo swaying in the breeze. Never had I suspected the charm attached to twinkling flashes of embroidery beneath a paneled, many-plaited skirt. My own number-four feet assumed alarming proportions. I grew positively ashamed of them. One day as Mother and I sat together in armchairs, with a blackwood tea-table between us, I placed my feet in line with hers and said, sighing, "Ah, they look very bad, indeed!" She waved a deprecating hand. "Never mind," she said with courtesy and truth; "they may not look so well, but they certainly walk better."

Of course I was glad that the small Alicia belonged to Young China, and would purchase no golden lilies with a cask of tears, as I had often read that every woman with bound feet must do. But I now decided that the cask must have been filled in the years of girlhood. For the women about me seemed to suffer no pain—only an occasional numbness, relieved by brisk massage from knee to ankle under the hands of a maid. I was surprised at the ease and energy with which they got about, merely balancing with small forward and backward steps when stopping—unless they had a servant's arm, or a cane, for support.

I thought our mother infinitely superior in the grace and dignity of her carriage. Madame Springtime, who had slightly enlarged her feet, at the command of her husband, moved slowly and with a lack of grace characteristic of the younger generation. Madame Chang moved ponderously and with difficulty. Madame Chau hurried with quick, fluttering steps. On occasion she would even run races with Alfred, our merry second son, now two-and-one-half years old. She would catch his hand, lean forward and hurry him the length of the hall, the two of them laughing gaily. Now and then I would fold my hands, balance on my heels and essay a "willow walk," to the great amusement of Mother and Madame Chau.

Life went very evenly for me in my Chinese mother's house after my husband's departure. His father had not come home for his semi-annual visit, and the second son was away again. Even the quiet-mannered third son, who looked just like his mother, and who used to bring me roses from the garden every day, had sailed for the island port to take his place in the family business. We were under a benevolent matriarchate in the snug compound among the brown hills now brightening to springtime green.

Madame Liang was infallibly generous and kind. I never heard her speak sharply except occasionally to servants who had by their carelessness caused something to go amiss, impeding the smooth progress of daily family life. I used to watch her with interest as she directed the household affairs from the throne of her great bed. She rarely gave her orders at first hand, but would summon a relative or an upper servant, who would receive and pass them down to those for whom they were intended. This imparted to her orders an empress-like finality and importance. The servants gave her complete allegiance.

She took great pride in conducting me through the complicated structure where generations of Liangs had lived and died. Extending back from the main establishment was a series of smaller ones like it, each with its own courtyard, its main hall containing the family altar, its private chambers opening on each side. Similar chains of "homes within a home" extended east and west, at right angles to this central chain. Mother showed me the rooms she had occupied as a bride, with the chamber where Chan-King was born, when the older Madame Liang ruled affairs with a firm yet kindly hand. I felt deeply moved by all this, more than ever a part of the family.

I made many small mistakes, I know, in my effort to practice the toleration, industry and courtesy exemplified in that family group, but Mother, unlike many of the oversensitive, easily offended Chinese women of her class, was divinely patient. She never asked of me anything that she deemed unfitting for me and she showed a wise discrimination in all the small tasks she assigned. I sometimes accompanied her to the temple, or to the ancestral graves, but only as a spectator. Her religious toleration required no compromise. She wanted me to see where grandparents and great-grandparents were laid to rest. She knew I was interested and filled with respect. To Madame Springtime fell the task of caring for the family altar and keeping up the daily devotions before the sacred shrine.

This young wife was in every way so typical of the old-fashioned Chinese woman, trained but not educated, disciplined but not broken, that I found her a continual source of interest. She was naturally shy and silent, but after a time we talked a little, and one day she showed me her bridal trunks of white lacquer with red and gold decorations, filled to the top with her bridal finery, exquisitely folded, and the clothes for her first child, which had been provided by her parents as a part of her wedding outfit.

This latter custom of Chan-King's native province appealed to me. It was typical of the many simplicities I found among my adopted people. Those small, brilliant-colored garments of padded silk and brocade and linen were symbols of hope, good omens for happiness and a fruitful marriage. Accustomed as I was to falsely puritanic ideals concerning the important realities of life—marriage and birth—their frank attitude toward fundamentals, their unquestioning acceptance of the facts of existence came as a pleasant surprise to me.

I liked also the curious contrast between their simple view of the elemental things and the formality and rigor of their personal etiquette. It is the manner of an old and ever cultivated race, who have long since ceased building at the foundation and are now occupied with the decorations of life.

Their scheme of daily living is based on the firm belief that the normal mode of human existence is family life. To this end it must be preserved at any cost. Life cannot develop in discord. If the amenities are worth anything at all, they are worth preserving constantly and at whatever personal sacrifice.

Life behind the arched gate was so pleasant and so filled with small, daily occupations that I thought little of going about. The village had no theater. On festal days performances were given by traveling troupes, on temporary stages, in temples or private houses. But we occasionally attended the theater in the great city near by, and, when we had guests staying with us for several days, they sometimes accompanied us. We were rather an impressive sight, I fancy, borne at a brisk trot, in half a dozen sedan-chairs, down the irregular path at dusk, preceded and followed by men servants carrying lanterns.

The children led a sheltered, happy existence, with servants and young relatives to amuse them indoors or without, as the weather permitted. They were liberally supplied, by their indulgent grandmother, with pocket-money in the form of handfuls of coppers instead of the strings of cash that sufficed an earlier generation. From passing vendors they bought bows and arrows of brightly painted bamboo, whistling birds and theatrical figures of colored earthenware, inflated rubber toys and an endless variety of rice-flour cakes, sesame-seed confections, peanut taffy and millet candy. On festal days the choice was wider than ever, with fluffy bunches of sugar wool (fine-spun syrup) and brittle candy toys blown from molten taffy with all the glass-blower's art, in the form of lanterns, birds and fish, mounted on slender sticks. At certain seasons, there were huge fish made of bamboo frames, paper-covered and realistically painted, which swam in a breeze with lazy grace, or kites similarly fashioned to represent birds and dragons, which winged upward in fascinating flight.

There was a limited foreign settlement in this same city and several of the American and British women came to call on me. Some of them were frankly curious to know how I had come through the "ordeal by family," as one of them expressed it, though of course they were very tactful.

Mother was much interested in these visitors, many of whom—if able to speak Chinese—I presented to her. When they left, she would often ask questions as to their nationality, their husbands' occupation, the number of their children. As for that question, most of them confessed to one child or, occasionally, two. But I shall never forget the call of a strikingly handsome, auburn-haired woman and the conversation that followed her departure. In reply to the usual inquiry, I said, "No children at all! But she has five *dogs* and has just bought, in Shanghai, two more, which are coming down on the next steamer."

"No children at all, and five—*seven dogs!*" said Mother in tones of horror. And then we burst out laughing. But quickly she sobered. "Foreign women do not care for children," she said.

"I do," I protested. "I like many children."

"You," said my mother with a smile, "are a Chinese wife."

But happily my next caller was a sweet-faced American woman, the proud mother of six, two of whom she brought with her. So our national reputation was saved.

In these days, I thought a great deal about intermarriage as a problem. Back in Shanghai, a returned student who visited in our home for several days had said to Chan-King afterward, "I almost married an American girl while I was in college. I wish now I had been brave enough to do so." At that time I felt very sorry for the unknown girl who had missed all the happiness that was coming to me, and now I was more sure than ever of the true quality of my happiness. There was no doubt at all on that score. But I realized the many, many ways in which everything might have been spoiled. Had my husband been less considerate, less sincere and loyal, had his family been less kindly and broadminded, had I myself been capricious and willful or unable to adapt myself to surroundings, I might every day have plumbed the depths of misery. I decided

that no rules could be made about intermarriage. It was an individual problem, as indeed all marriage must be. So, when a young girl back home in
America wrote to me for advice, believing herself in love with a Chinese class-
mate, and concluded, "You, Mrs. Liang, must settle the question for me," I
answered, as I should not have done a year earlier: "That is a question that you
two alone are competent to settle. No one can advise you safely, for a mistake
either way may result in lifelong unhappiness. But I might venture to suggest
that love strong enough to stand the test of intermarriage does not seek advice.
It is sure of itself."

In a household where only my eldest son and I spoke English, my lingual
struggles were unexpectedly mild. Chan-King had left me a list of everyday
phrases, and my ear grew very keen in my constant efforts to understand the
rapid speech going on around me all day long. In a short while I could understand virtually everything said to me.

During the long conversations that Mother and I had in the quiet of the
evening, we talked much of Chan-King and she displayed treasured relics of
his boyhood: a small jacket of deep red velvet, a worn cap, a silver toy and the
identical schoolbook in which he began the study of English. I loved them all,
loved her the more for cherishing them and was made supremely happy by
being given a photograph of Chan-King at an earlier age than any he possessed. She was very much interested in all our photographs, too. She was
vastly amused at Chan-King arrayed for college theatricals and, when I
brought out pictures of myself at all ages, of my parents and grandparents, she
traced family resemblances with unerring perception.[1] Sometimes we looked
at magazines that Chan-King sent us from the capital or talked of various foreign customs. I soon found it very easy to talk with her and with her help I
learned also to read and write simple Chinese characters, for a very liberal-
minded father had given her educational advantages enjoyed by few girls of
her generation.

When the hands of her small ebony clock pointed to twelve, she would
touch my hand gently and say, "Time for you to sleep."

"But first I must write to Chan-King," I would answer.

She would shake her finger at me with kindly caution. "It is too late," she
would answer. "You must sleep."

I would hold out firmly on this point. "But my mother, if I do not write to
Chan-King, I cannot sleep!"

She would assent then, and next day I would carry the pages to show her,
for my letters to Chan-King and his voluminous responses were a source of

much amusement to her. I translated these letters to her as faithfully as my limited Chinese would allow, and in my letters always added messages dictated by her.

I was learning the romanized method of writing Chinese, which for our dialect has been remarkably developed and standardized. Mother was much interested when I showed her how to write familiar words with foreign letters, and Chan-King always answered these messages in kind, though his mother and he carried on a regular correspondence in the Chinese characters.

"Those children write long letters to each other, fifteen and twenty pages at a time," she often told her friends with manifest delight.

Beyond this personal companionship with my mother, which I enjoyed very much, there was no restraint put upon me in any way. I was free to walk out alone, to return calls and to shop in the city.

My own sense of fitness prompted me always to present myself at the door of my mother's apartment before I left the house, to explain to her the nature of my errand and to ask for her approval. Accepting the little formality for the courtesy it was, she never once demurred. She was accustomed to this respect, and I saw no reason for withholding it. All the invitations I received from acquaintances, either foreign or Chinese, I declined or accepted as she advised, because I relied upon her unfailing knowledge of people and social customs.

Twice during those months of Chan-King's absence death came near. Once it was a clever young boy, an only son, in whom high hopes had been centered; and then, the young girl who had accompanied Mother to Shanghai. She was no servant in the ordinary sense, but an orphaned distant relative of Mother's. Madame Liang was always kind and generous with her, and when, soon after her return from the trip to Shanghai, which had been a great event in her quiet life, a promising marriage offer was made, she was sent forth to her new home with a complete bridal outfit. Hearing at last of our presence in the family home, she put on her wedding-dress of pale green and came to see me. Her evident pleasure in the meeting touched me poignantly. With bright eagerness she told me of her husband, her kind mother-in-law. With pride she described her tiny son. After a gay hour with the children she left, promising to come again. But I never saw her afterward. Death took her abruptly from her happiness.

I began to think of death as something not so remote after all. Several times a group of us—children and cousins and friends and servants—made short chair-trips into the hills. The sight of thousands of graves, their stones whitening the hillsides for miles in some places, impressed me more and more with the comparative shortness of life.

Scattered over many of these hills are curious monuments of stone, called "widow arches," each one standing alone, usually by a roadside, in commemoration of a faithful wife who, in ancient days, killed herself at the death of her husband. A widow who wished to make this sacrifice would, after a short lapse of time, announce her intention of committing suicide. The members of her family would erect a high stage for her and invite relatives and friends to attend the ceremony. At the chosen hour, the lady would hang herself, and a high stone arch would later be erected as a memorial of her devotion and heroism.

In the Chinese family, the widow who does not remarry receives honor and veneration second only to the mother-in-law. With age, she acquires added authority. She is not forbidden to remarry, but the conditions of second marriage are made difficult enough to discourage any but the most intrepid. The children of her first husband remain in the house of his people, and the family of her second husband do not give her any too cordial a welcome.

One naturally prefers free will in these things. Yet I had a whole-hearted sympathy with the idea of life-widowhood, long before I dreamed it was to be my portion. Painful as the sight of the "widow arches" was to me at first, my convictions made the Chinese view of them seem not unnatural, though I knew the custom had been forbidden by imperial edict some two centuries earlier.

Even in the days when Chan-King and I believed that our love would somehow give us earthly immortality, the idea was strong in me that to those who loved truly, death could only extinguish the torch for a moment to relight it in the clearer flame of eternity. Then, I cherished this thought in the background of my mind. Now, I live by it.

For this reason, too, I have always found the Chinese attitude toward the dead very comforting. They never for a moment relinquish hold on their loved ones. The death-day anniversary is as festal an occasion as the day of birth. The pageant of life marches without a break, birth to death and beyond, and birth again, the generations endlessly touching mystical hands, until the individual feels himself to be part of an endless procession that passes for a moment into a white light and out again, feels himself touching those who came before and those who come after—one of a long line, bound together irrevocably.

With all their ethics of personal sacrifice and their preoccupation with the idea of eternity, the Chinese have no ascetic contempt for the material world and they earnestly desire and seek length of days. Among the varied symbols and characters used to express good wishes—as health, honor, riches—those for "long life" hold preeminence. They are wrought in rings, bracelets, hair ornaments, and are sewed into bridal garments and upon children's little coats and caps. I always felt this enormous respect for life in all their daily customs—the preparing of the baby clothes when the bride left her father's house, the nurturing and strengthening of the clan with many children, the reverent regard for the graves of the ancestors to whom the living owed their grace of existence.

On several occasions I accompanied my mother on her visits to the ancestral graves. I remember the last time, only a few days before Chan-King's return, that I walked with her, holding one of her hands, while with the other she grasped her gold-headed cane. She wore a light costume—a plaited black skirt and lavender "coat" and lovely black kid shoes. Servants followed with her baskets of offerings.

We stood at a respectful distance, in silence, while she performed her rites. All about were placed papers, weighted down with small stones. She knelt and, clasping her hands, devoutly repeated her prayers under her breath. Then, assisted by a servant, she burned the paper symbols of refreshment and replenishment for the dead. Firecrackers were exploded to clear the air of evil spirits, and the ceremony was over.

As we returned to the village, everywhere people called out to her from their doorways and she invariably replied with friendly courtesy. In the outskirts we stopped for rest and a visit at the home of a cousin. When we left, many of the relatives and friends went with us a little way, crying out repeatedly, "Good-by!" and "Come again, come again soon!" I saw the sunlight on Tiger Mountain; I smelled the saltiness of the sea. As we passed around the great boulders that hid them from our sight, the modulated cadence of their "Come again, come again soon!" floated to us. It was the last time I should hear it as I was then, and I did not even dream that it was so.

For a month I had been expecting the arrival of Chan-King. His letters were always love-letters, with added paragraphs saying that he was getting on well with his work and would have much to tell me of it when he came home. At last a letter told us to expect him by a certain steamer, on a certain day. But schedules were still in confusion because of the war. That steamer was delayed, and Chan-King sailed for another port, meaning to change there. More delays followed. More letters of explanation. More delays again. Mother and I both became heart-sick with hope deferred. At last, one morning, worn out with watching, I slept later than usual, and on that morning Chan-King came home.

Awakened out of a long drowse, I heard a stir in the quiet house, the clang of a gong, a rush of padded footfalls in the outer hall. Happy voices mingled in greeting at the door of my mother's apartment. I threw on my robe, tucked Alicia under my arm and ran across the room, flinging the door open even as Chan-King had his hand raised to knock at the panel. I saw him dimly in the wavering light. He was smiling, and behind him stood his mother, also smiling. Each of us solemnly spoke the other's name, trying to erase, with a long look, the memory of all those months of absence. Then he saw the baby. "Li-Sia, my thousand catties of gold!" he said, in Chinese. Alicia smiled and held out her arms to him. "She recognizes him!" said Mother, in pleased surprise. We three stood together a moment, silently, gathered around the child. I felt myself more deeply absorbed into the clan—a Chinese woman, dedicated anew, heart and spirit, to my adopted people.

Later, Chan-King explained to me the reason for his home-coming. His legal service for the government had been completed and his expected appointment had come at last. We were to return to America, where he would be in the Chinese consular service.[2] After a period in this work, a bright future in the diplomatic field seemed assured. It meant leaving my beloved China, where I had firmly taken root. But we agreed that the exile would be for only a few years and that we would return surely to our Promised Land, there to enjoy our span of "long life with honor."

Now our leisurely existence was broken up to a degree. Almost immediately we set about preparations for our new life in America. Chan-King looked forward with absorbing interest to the change, almost as if he were going home. My instant reaction was one of joy, swiftly followed by sorrow at giving up things now loved and familiar. I wanted to appear cheerful, as a duty to those around me. I did not want to seem too cheerful, lest Mother think me glad to go.

In this period, at last, I met my Chinese father. One beautiful day in early autumn, Chan-King and I went down to the city, returning in mid-afternoon. As our chairs were set down before the entrance, the gatekeeper announced to Chan-King his father's arrival. I was filled with swift apprehension. Again chance had decided my costume: I was wearing—not the conservative Chinese garb in which I had met my mother—but a frilly American dress of blue and white summer silk, a white lace hat with black velvet and pink rosebuds and white kid pumps. Chan-King had on white flannels and a Panama hat. The latter he handed to a servant, as also his cane. As we entered the main room together, a figure rose from beside Mother to receive us. I saw an elderly man of medium height, with grim, smooth-shaven face and gray hair. He was wearing a long gown of deep blue silk, with a black outer jacket and the usual round cap of black satin. My husband first greeted him and then presented me. While I stood uncertain, there was a courteous inclination of the gray head, the grimness of expression dissolved in a wonderfully winning smile, and, surprisingly, as Mother had done, my Chinese father extended his hand. I felt that he was interpreting me in the light of all she had told him, that his cordial handclasp and kindly words of welcome were his ratification of her judgment. Then, with a courtly gesture, he assigned me to his lately occupied chair beside Mother, while he and Chan-King took seats together opposite us. Mother smiled into my eyes with her happiest expression. I felt that Chan-King's background was complete. Long before, I had conceived of it as harsh and threatening, but I had now proved it to be wholly kind and protecting. At my recent fear of this last test I wondered and smiled.

Father was much gratified at finding his grandsons able to converse fluently in his native speech. He would gather them all about him for an hour at a time, asking questions to test their practical knowledge, or telling stories to amuse them. Alicia also delighted him. At simple Chinese commands, she would now clasp her hands or fold them and bow profoundly. Mother was very proud of her wee granddaughter and would often say, "She is just as Chan-King was at her age!" And her husband would invariably assent with an indulgent smile. There existed between these two—conservative types though they were—an evidence of mutual affection and respect, of real companionship, that touched me profoundly. I was glad that Father was to be with Mother when Chan-King and I took ourselves and our three children from the home where, according to the old Chinese custom, we all rightfully belonged.

The question of leaving one or more of our children there for a time was discussed one afternoon later.

"Under ordinary circumstances," said Father to Chan-King, "you would go alone, as your brother does, leaving your entire family with us. At the very least, you would allow one child to remain in your stead. But, of course, your mother and I understand that these are not ordinary circumstances. Your wife is an American. She has been considerate of our point of view in many ways— more than we expected—and in this matter we do not fail to consider hers, which is no doubt your own as well. We understand that according to the American view the children belong with their parents, always. We cannot, of course, deny your right to this manner of living. But we want you to feel that, if you can leave even one child with us, we shall be very happy. You understand what protection and care will be given it."

For a moment there was silence. My heart was very full, and, even had it been my place to speak, I should have been unable to do so. Mentally I pictured Mother's loneliness at losing so many of her children. Vainly I tried to imagine our home in America with even one small face missing. I watched my husband, noted the tiny traces of conflict in his face, impassive perhaps to the casual glance. At last he spoke.

"Father, Mother," he began earnestly, "we do indeed appreciate your great kindness and generosity. You will understand that, just as you understand most truly our situation. We know that here with you our children would have many advantages that we, perhaps, cannot give them. But which one could we leave to enjoy those advantages? Not Wilfred, for he is our eldest son, on whom we place great dependence. And Alfred—of us all he seems least fitted for the southern climate. The summer heat has left him a little pale and listless. He needs the sea voyage. As for Alicia, she is the baby, and our only daughter. Do not think us unmindful of all you have done. But I fear we should not know how to make our home without our children."

After all, it was evidently not unexpected. They shook their heads a trifle ruefully at each other and then smiled.

"Very well," Father assented. "But this you must promise: that at intervals, whenever your work permits, you will come back—all of you—and spend a year with us again. Do not let the children forget us nor their Chinese speech. In four years, at most, all come back together."

We promised readily, Mother and I repeating the phrase to each other, "In four more years, all come back together." Our eyes were full of tears.

That night I said to my husband, "We should have left one of them."

But Chan-King was a clearer thinker, just then, and knew the truth of this situation better than I did. "Which one?" he asked me, significantly, in a tone that made me see the essential hollowness of my protest.

On the Sunday before our ship sailed, Chan-King and I bade farewell to China. In company with our parents and many other relatives we walked to the top of a very high hill, where an old temple, which commanded a magnificent view for miles around, crouched contentedly among the rocks, in the gray sunshine. It was a temple of the three religions, with huge stone images of Confucius, Buddha and Lao-tse grouped in its outer court. Together, Chan-King and I climbed to the crest of the terraced rock. I looked about me, down upon the proud, bright little village, alert and colorful on the hillside, upon the scattering fertile patches in the midst of the barren mountains where tigers build their lairs. The eternal hills swept the lowering, clouded skies, rolling away from us, silent, shadow-filled. A surging love of the very soil under my feet, a clinging to the earth of China, overwhelmed me. I wished to kneel down and kiss that beloved dust. "Oh, Chan-King," I said, shaking with emotion, "This is home! I wish we were not leaving, even for a day!"

"We will come again soon," he said, in Chinese, "and we will live here when we are old."

That evening we sat together in the quiet garden. From Mother's apartments came the sound of her young nephew's voice as he chanted his morrow's lessons. We heard the subdued merriment of two little maids, teasing each other in the hall beyond. Along the outer path a sedan-chair passed with rhythmic sway, the bamboo supports creaking a soft accompaniment to the pad-pad of the bearers' sandaled feet.

From varying distances came the clang of a brass gong, shuddering on the stillness, the staccato sound of slender bamboo sticks shaken together in a cylindrical box, the measured beat of a small drum-rattle, as the different street vendors announced their wares. Over the hills, now purple in twilight, the round moon swung leisurely into the violet sky. Strange breaths of incense wafted about us. The sea-breeze stirred the branches of a nearby dragon's-eye tree, where the ripening fruit-balls tapped gently against each other like little swaying lanterns. For long moments we sat in silence, with clasped hands.

Out of that silence my husband spoke softly, words I had long yearned to hear: "Absence, Margaret, teaches many things. Once it showed you your own heart. This time it has taught me to believe with you in the immortality of love like ours. Physically, we may be separated at times, but mentally, spiritually, you and I are one for all eternity." The moon rose higher, golden, perfect, even as our love.

A few days later, we sailed for America. The rest may be told in a few words, for after all, no words could adequately tell it. A week after our arrival in America, Chan-King was stricken with influenza. For several years he had been in the shadow of a slow illness, but with stout resistance and such buoyant recurring periods of good health that we had for a time almost forgotten that early and sinister threat. But those years of struggle were all thrown into the balance against him when the decisive hour came. After six days, he died.[3] Quietly, with terrible implacability, death closed over him. We feared a sudden end, it is true, but were still incredulous of such a calamity. We gave each other what assurance we could: our ultimate farewells were simple renewals of faith, a firmer tightening of our hands for our walk in darkness. "Of all the world, you are my love," he said, many times. "More than anyone else you have understood, you have been unfailing—you have been my wife." And almost as he spoke, my arms held no longer my living beloved, but only the clay where his spirit had been and would come no more.

So, by the visible evidences, my history is finished. But it has begun anew for me, not as I wished, not as I hoped, but on a level that I can endure. For I have my children and my memories and my home in China, which waits with the gentle healing of sight and sound and place . . . and I have learned that in love, and only in love, we can wring spiritual victory out of this defeat of the body.

APPENDIX
Letters and Newspaper Accounts

Mae Watkins to herself, 29 August 1909, to be opened 29 August 1910. A flower was enclosed and the letter sealed.

Aug. 29, 1909
10:30 P.M.

O what a beautiful afternoon—what an exquisite evening! And now the end is come.—Now he is gone. I have listened till the sound of his footstep died away into the night,.and beyond that I have watched until the last dark outline of his figure merged into the shadow. Now that last blessed moment has passed like the others.—Now I sit here alone—alone with the quietness of the night and my thots, that never on any other night can be just as they are now. In vain I try to analyze them—peaceful, sorrowful, calm or happy—I cannot say. Not entirely peaceful, tho in my heart has come with this last day a brief new peace; not entirely sorrowful for the sweet blessedness of giving and receiving dispels grief; not calm, tho something strangely benumbing which must soon pass away; not happy for the sadness of even such a parting must needs tinge the joy.

And what a strange parting! How different from what I had looked forward to and taught myself to expect! How infinitely dearer! No rash promises, made but to be broken, no impossible declarations—but instead simple statements of what has been, and simple hopes of what may be,—simple, yet implying so much,—and more than all that—which I cannot regret, try as I may. No I cannot be sorry for it, and wish it undone, for tis—it was—"the last time,"—and we both understand.

Ah, how much this means to me now! It has taken all the first bitterness out of the parting and given me an assurance which is sweet and comforting now,—now when I need it most. After that its briefness——, ah, that is the true point, indeed!

Just now, at this present moment, it means so much to me, and I know as truly that it means as much to him. But a year from this day—how will it then appear to both of us?—As something to be forgotten, or as a sweet memory, cherished still, perhaps, as a hope—a "low of promise"—for the future?

Ah, well, a year from now and I shall answer easily—it will not matter then. But ah, the interval between!

219 S. Ingalls St.
Ann Arbor, Michigan
December 10, 1909

Dear friend Tiam,—

. . . . I wish to feel that you are as truly my friend now as when we were daily associated, and that you will still be the same when, in a few years again, we are separated by many more miles than now lie between us. For my part, I know that I shall always be interested in you, ready to rejoice at your successes, and to regret should misfortune come. Thus I think we can always be friends in spirit, if we are to justify the time and attention which we have already devoted to it. . . .

There is a constantly growing admiration and respect for China and for the Chinese people here in this country. I hope you are proud that the opportunity is yours to further such a feeling. I am glad, too, that you are not giving your whole attention to school work; what you will gain from those outside matters will be worth far more to you later on than mere book-learning. . . .

Is it very cold in Grand Rapids now? We are beautifully frosted here in old A. A.

I remain as ever, Mae

195 Lyon St.
Grand Rapids, Mich.
April 15, 1910

Dear Mae:

I feel entirely satisfied from the explanation you have given me in your letter of last week, and the expressed love in the one of this week. You may be sure that both of your tender and kind letters have made me very happy. . . . I am very glad to receive the confession of your sincere attachment and will not attempt to conceal how truly I return it, and how earnestly I shall endeavor to prove worthy of your devotion. In fact, I feel sure, some way, that there is a perfect understanding and sympathy between us. Not only from your words but also from your deeds. I have believed, for some time, that you care for me;—how could I think otherwise. . . .

Still, I shall look with some anxiety for the assurance that I have not misunderstood your feelings and that you return my affection.

Goodbye, my dearest, and let me hold thee to my heart.

I am, yours lovingly,
Tiam

219 South Ingalls,
Ann Arbor, Michigan
April 22, 1910

Dear Tiam,—

Your last letter came to me on Monday, and I have read it thru very carefully, not once, but many times. Yet how shall I answer it? Just what shall I say to you in reply?

First, let me explain that I truly did not realize just how much I had been telling you. That I should have done so is hardly in accordance with my own ideas of a woman's part. . . . Yet, that I have almost unconsciously given you reasons for believing that I care for you, does not make the fact itself any the less true,—perhaps it is even further proof of it.

For, since you have asked, and if I would still be loyal to myself and to you, I cannot deny that which I now know to be true beyond a doubt,—tho indeed, the full realization of it has only recently come to me. No, you did not misunderstand. In fact, I sometimes think that perhaps you have understood better than I. But because you have told me of your own feelings for me, and if it will make you any happier now to know directly, then—Tiam, I love you. . . .

Now I must say "good-bye" . . . with my love, Mae

917 E. Huron St.
Ann Arbor, Mich.
July 27, 1910

My dear girl,—

I received your long-look[ed]-for letter this morning and I can not tell you how glad I am to know that you are happy and are enjoying your vacation immensely. . . . Now, I must not take all the time to answer the questions, for there are quite good deal of thots that I wish to express here to you.

After all, I think we all have the same kind of feeling for one another, or in other words we seem to understand our feelings pretty well. For this reason, I am happy and, indeed, I am thankful to have been endowed with a heart capable of feeling and knowing the immense value of beauty and comfort. Do you know, dearest, that your letters were very satisfactory and conclusive to me in every way; . . . also by reason of the immeasurable intensity of affection therein? Truly, tho happiness that is not spoken of, is in its nature the most sacred & secret. Then, how clear it is that love which is found on comfort and happiness, is, indeed, richer than wealth and nobler than name. Beyond any rational doubt, dearest, you have drawn my whole heart.

I remain yours, Tiam

[26 October 1910, letter Mae wrote to one of her aunts.]

.... *But, here I don't mean to preach, for you have been very sweet to me, when all my relatives and friends here have read me lectures on my duty to my parents, my country, my flag and—yes, even to my future children,—all this as tho the day were set, the guests invited, and the minister engaged. Well, I believe I am deeply sensible of my duty in all cases,—most especially to the last mentioned, but perhaps I see that duty in a different light,—in addition, I recognize a duty to myself and to him, which they will not, or cannot see. Uncle Pete and Aunt Mae were here last week, & I met more "stone walls." But I shall not attempt to batter them down and run the risk of dashing out my poor brains. There is a way around, and I shall follow that if possible. Just now the future is so far away. I have not yet finished my high school work, and beyond that the university lies before me.*

However, what they think and say and do does not bother me for I will prepare myself . . . and accept that which does *come as right. If it be the fulfillment of my dearest hopes there will even then be enough of sorrow to make it serious enough, and if it be disappointment I shall strive to blame no one, receiving it as the decision of "One who knoweth best, and who doeth all things well."*

Mae

611 E. Liberty St.
Ann Arbor, Mich.
March 17, 1911

"My Tiam,"—

I was surprised, and oh, so very, very pleased this afternoon to receive your dear pin and loving words which accompanied it. It is lovely, I think, and very dear to me already—for it is a Michigan *seal pin and just the kind I have admired and wanted for a long time. . . .*

Dearest, the very force which has led you to doubt, however slightly, is the force which makes and keeps my love for you faithful and deep and pure. This force does guide me in all things and I know it guides you, too, for it must guide the life of every true man and woman. Yet it is individual between each one and the Creator of all,—as the rainbow is individual between each person and the sun, and no one may quite see or understand clearly that of another. Understand! Oh, my Dear,—there is a fact which education impresses upon us ever more and more as we penetrate farther into all its different branches. It is this: we cannot understand perfectly and completely anything in all this universal world. It was not meant that we should, I think. But we can have faith *and* trust,—*how much more so where* love *already is. Yes, and we shall have happiness,—for when Love, Faith and Trust rule happiness must come.*

Oh, my Tiam consider all these, and put aside thy doubts and fears. I love thee, and my heart is thine unto death, and beyond, unto eternity, if God choose.

(And weeks never can be made months or years, not in the way you have feared.)

Oh, dearest, I have thot all day and my heart has been sad, but your sweet gift and all it means has brot peace into my heart, and surcease from pain. So with these words I send sincerest gratitude and thanks, and God grant that these thots may bring you peace and comfort. . . .

Lovingly your Mae

611 E. Liberty St.
Ann Arbor, Mich.
June 16, 1911

My dear Tiam,—

I have read your letter again and again, and I do not think I misunderstand, but in reply I can say nothing more than what I have already repeated many, many times, for the thots of my heart have always been an open book to you.

Dear Boy, I know you are not well, for otherwise things would not appear to you in such a light. And, dearest, again I beg of you to go to your doctor and take his advice, which is precious, but for the sake of all other things. Then all will be right.

Oh Tiam, life to me is a dreary wilderness of pain, and every nerve quivers with the torture of it all. Even as I write this letter the hot tears burn my eyes cold tho it may seem to you at the threatened ruin of our dearest hopes. . . .

Lovingly,
Mae

611 E. Liberty St.
A. A. Mich.
June 18, 1911

My dearest Tiam,—

There are so many things I want to tell you, dear, and talk over with you. But I could not say anything over the phone, could not hear all you were saying, and did not know how to answer you.

Dearest, my silence does not mean that I have peace. Oh, peace is very far from my struggling heart and soul in these hours, and the pain is many times greater because you, too, are suffering.

Oh Tiam, believe me, my love is still there: that it is unchanged, even tho you cannot see it, and I am fully conscious of the effort you are making to bring things out alright. Dear, will you make one further effort? Acknowledge to yourself that things may not be as they now appear *to you; admit that my* seeming *lack of love may be due to some other cause than that I have not been sincere, and come to me, willing to hear my cause before you judge in darkness and condemn unjustly one who has given you the deepest, the purest affection that a woman's heart and soul can know, and who is still, as ever, lovingly yours,*

Mae

Ft. Wayne, Indiana
July 5th, 1911

My dearest Mae,—

    Everything resolves into this. I deeply regret acting as I did; but you are so good & gentle, I am sure you will receive me into favor on my writing you this. You must not be very angry with me for fearing to lose what I prize so dearly, the love of my darling Mae. . . . It has been too much for me & made me shed tears many times & I have no heart to do anything. It is so hard to doubt one you love, & it seems that I have tormented myself quite unnecessarily all these past weeks; still you must admit there was something for my making myself miserable & yet you can't see it—I am convinced. Oh, what was I to think of your silence & what you have done happily! Dearest Mae, don't lose hope, I beg of you. There is something that seems to haunt me so long ago, there is something in your charms so sweet that captured me so long, and I like you, because you are different from all other girls I know!

    If I don't hear, however, from you I shall consider everything ends right here, for there is nothing so worse as to drag things. . . .

Yours,
Tiam

611 E. Liberty St.
Ann Arbor, Mich.
July 6, 1911

My dearest Tiam,—

    I wish that I might express to you how your letter has lightened the ache in my heart, and turned the sad weariness of these last days into hope. . . .

    Ah, my Tiam, there has been pain in my heart,—all the deeper pain because I knew that you, too, were suffering, and I seemed so powerless to alter things in any way. Dear, all thru this last year I have suffered more than you, perhaps, can understand, in my vain attempt to make over my will unto yours, and to change my unalterable convictions. The result of my year's endeavor came in this last month. I had tried so hard, dear to see things as I knew you saw them and to meet your demands, but I could not. I thot and thot continually, until finally my mind just gave out—from sheer mental exhaustion—and I was utterly incapable of acting, or thinking, or even of feeling deeply. I sank into an apathy, and this was at a time when my work at school demanded attention most imperatively. That work I did in a sort of subconscious way, but I can truthfully say that never in all my life have I seen—nor do I expect to see—days of greater torture. I often wondered how I could live from one day to the next and do what was expected of me. . . . And all this time I realized that you also were suffering most keenly, torturing yourself, oh, so needlessly! with the thot that I no longer cared for you. Your very efforts to compel me only drove me farther into my horrible seclusion in spite of myself, for you were so unlike my boy. Tiam, I do not believe you can realize how different you were. Dearest! Dearest! . . .

The past has held many dear associations for us, and we have had fair hopes for the future. But, Tiam, irrespective of all that has been, or of all that may be, I must do now what my heart tells me is right. I have tried for your sake to silence its voice, but in vain, and for your sake still I must now heed it. Yes, dear, if a girl loves a man she wants him—as I love you and want you—I do agree with you in that. But I cannot accept the opinion that you have expressed that if a girl loves a man she will forget everything and be willing to sacrifice everything "for the sake of love." True love in its broad compass is all, I do believe, but the narrow passion we so often term "love" is only one arc of the perfect [circle] and must never attempt to become all. If a girl values herself so little that she can yield all to the passion of the moment and sacrifice all "for the sake of love," do you think that, as a wife, should temptation come to her—and it comes to us all, perhaps, at times—do you think that then she would suddenly understand the value of her husband's honor and her own? If she were true to her nature she would again sacrifice all "for the sake of love," and how much more the all would mean now than before. Oh, Tiam, is this your ideal! I cannot think so.

The true woman who knows the value of all things, no matter how deeply she may love a man, until the time when she's bound to him by the sacred ties of marriage will consider herself above all things else,—not her selfish self, made up of whims and caprices which avail nothing, but her most sacred self, the self which she hopes to give into the keeping of her husband alone. And he may rest with a contented mind, knowing that she will guard his honor as sacredly as she has kept her own. Is this your ideal! I trust that it may be, for between these two there is no sure medium.

Tiam, God has made me a woman, and the birthright of a pure mind and true *heart combined with years of training have made me what you now find me,—whether worthy or unworthy in my Creator's sight I cannot know. But however that may be, I am as I am, and my earnest attempt to change radically my principles and very conception of right and wrong have ended in failure. I cannot change them. They are stronger, firmer than ever for this brief subjection. But as you love me for myself alone and for what I am, you will not ask me to change them.*

Tiam, if you want a girl who will forget everything and be willing to serve you only in every way before marriage gives her the right, then I must disappoint you and myself. But if you want "a woman's love, a woman's arms, a woman's understanding tenderness"—then do I rejoice. For I love you Tiam,—God above knows how—and I am willing to give you my heart with its fullest loyalty and devotion, willing to share your pleasures, more than willing to share your sorrow, for I could almost desire them to be greater in number that I might have the joy of soothing them away and bringing you peace out of pain. This I long to give and with it the hope of some day giving all. And I ask of you that, besides your love,—or rather as a part of your love, you give me such trust and confidence that you can feel secure in my love for you, and that when I say "I cannot," you will now be content, knowing it is not a proof that I do not love you as I might, but rather a token that my love for you is of the kind you will want in the woman you make your wife. Ah Tiam, with this understanding between us our love would be founded upon the firm rocks indeed, and no earthly storms could ever shatter its sure foundation. Will you not grant me this! I ask it with a prayer to heaven that you may.

I could not have written these things to you had I not felt the strength of the tie that draws and binds us to each other. Even in these last few days I could not conquer the feeling that we belong to each other, that we are meant to be one. "Ah Love let us be true to one another." Be happy, dear, write soon and tell me that you understand, for I want to read your own words. And believe me ever most lovingly yours,

Mae

P.S. After all I have written do you not see, dear, that you must decide! It is not alone that I feel strongly on this subject. The feelings that I have here expressed are not my life only,—they are my immortal soul.

Mae

Mar. 29, 1912

My dearest Boy,—

I don't know how to write this, but I think you will understand.

I want to talk to you, Tiam, after this morning I begin to think it quite necessary that I should see you as soon as possible. Wont you come tonight, Dearest? I know you said you had to study, but you also said once—and more than once—that I meant more to you than your studies, and that when I needed you, you would be here.

Oh, dearest, aren't you near enough to my heart to feel the weary wilderness of pain that surrounds it? Only come, Dear, what I have to say cannot wait any longer.

Lovingly,
Mae

P. O. G. D.
Detroit, Michigan
Aug. 26, (P.M.) 1912

Dearest Mae,—

I don't care whether I am a good waiter or not—all I want is a chance to get some money & to complete my course of study.

Now—my plan amounted to this: (I think, tho I am not absolute certain) I shall take some studies in the after sessions at the Detroit College of Law & work from 6 to 12 P.M. . . . . I shall try to see the Dean or the secretary of the college tomorrow. . . . I can get $80.00 a month if not more & get thru my work in a year or two. . . .

Mae, dearest, I am glad I started the study of law. . . . Are you happy about my plans . . . outlined above?

Yours,
Tiam

From the Ann Arbor Times, *September 1912:*

CHINESE WEDS LOCAL WOMAN

Student From Amoy Marries a Co-ed in University of Michigan

Friends have just learned of the marriage of Miss May Watkins, daughter of Mr. and Mrs. H. O. Watkins of 611 East Liberty street, to a Chinese student, Tiam Franking of Amoy, China.

The marriage took place last Saturday, and the ceremony was performed by Rev. W. O. Raymond, curate of St. Andrew's Episcopal church, who consented to officiate after he had been assured that the young man was a Christian and after the parents of the girl had consented.

Miss Watkins was one of the prettiest and most popular girls in the high school. She is 21 years old and after completing her high school work she entered the literary department of the university. It was, however, in the high school that she met the young Chinaman, and a friendship almost at once sprang up and continued to grow more intimate in spite of the warnings of Miss Watkins' friends. At one time, [it] is said, her parents attempted to break up the affair, but they found that both young people were determined, and rather than become estranged from their daughter they finally gave their consent. The young bride declares that her husband has promised never to return to his native country unless his wife desires him to do so, and they plan to locate here in America after Mr. Franking has finished his college course. During the summer he was employed by a Detroit concern and he has asked to be transferred from the law department of the university where he has finished his junior year, to the Detroit law school, so that he may keep on with his work. He is 22 years old and is reported to be from a very wealthy family. Mrs. Franking at first planned to continue her work in the university but it is now likely that she will go to Detroit with her husband.

From the **Ann Arbor Times,** *September 1912:*

A CONCRETE REASON
FOR THE RACE PREJUDICE
AT ANN ARBOR.

The marriage in Ann Arbor of an American girl and a Chinese student brings acutely to the front one of the puzzling problems in connection with the matriculation of Oriental students at the University of Michigan. Much has been said and written in these last few months concerning the prevalence of race prejudice at the university, particularly in the case of the Hindoo students. Various causes have been assigned, ignorance and narrowness in particular, but those who have lived the college life and who still keep in touch with it are inclined to the belief that one great trouble is the fascination which the Orientals, wittingly or otherwise, exercise over the co-eds, and they argue that in colleges and universities where there is no co-education this sort of race prejudice does not develop.

This is all very plausible and reasonable. It is undeniable that, whether justifiable or not, there is a very widespread prejudice against close social intercourse or intermarriage between American girls and young men from the Orient. And as has happened in the Ann Arbor case, marriage frequently brings social ostracism for the bride. Some idea of the reasonableness of this attitude as a fixed and unchangeable idea may be gained when it is remembered that the marriage of an American man and a Japanese or Chinese or Hindoo girl creates little or no such furore, and is rather accounted a pleasurable social sensation, the bride, if she is pretty and attractive, being petted and feted.

Of course there is a difference in the two cases, because the bride as a rule follows her husband and becomes subject to his ideas on the marriage relation and often to the laws of his land concerning it. This also explains the prejudice which sometimes exists in the Orient against the marriage of native women and American men.

But we have wandered a little aside from the subject. For the point we wish particularly to make is that, however happy the couple just married in Ann Arbor may be in years to come, however well mated they may be, the fact remains that their union has probably complicated the problem of receiving and retaining foreign students at the university and it is not unlikely when the news of the wedding is spread abroad more than one father and mother may hesitate to send their daughter to an institution which is likely to provide the young woman an Oriental husband as well as an education.

From the **Grand Rapids Herald**, *13 September 1912:*

American Girl Becomes Bride of Chinaman Who Formerly Lived in Grand Rapids; Friends Peeved

ANN ARBOR, Mich., Sept. 13—This whole town is agog over a wedding that occurred last Sunday, and has just "leaked out." The marriage was that of a Chinese student in the University of Michigan, and an American girl, also a student of the university. The marriage took place at the home of the bride's parents in this city, and Rev. W. O. Raymond, curate of the Episcopal church, performed the ceremony.

The bride was Miss Mae Watkins, a 1915 literary student and the man whom she married was Tiam Franking, of Amoy, China, a junior law student and one of the law debaters, and a graduate of the Grand Rapids high school.

The marriage was the culmination of a romance that started several years ago, when Franking first came to this country and entered the Ann Arbor high school, in which Miss Watkins was then a student. From then till now, the pathway of Cupid has been beset with all sorts of obstacles.

At one time opposition on the part of Mr. and Mrs. Watkins was so great that it is said to have been the reason for Franking's leaving the city for a year during which he studied and graduate[d] from the Grand Rapids high school but when he came back, the intimacy was again taken up. It is said that the parents were finally won over to the marriage, rather than lose their daughter out of their lives.

Rev. Raymond tonight admitted that he had married the couple but stated that before doing so he had questioned the father and mother of the bride, and that they said to him, "personality counts more with us than does race," after that Rev. Raymond no longer hesitated to marry the couple.

The friends of the bride have tried for months to keep her from marrying the man, and have tried in every way to break off the friendship, but all to no avail. Even the unfortunate stories of other Ann Arbor girls who had married foreign students, were of no avail, for according to the bride, she is never to be obliged to live in China, nor in any foreign country if she does not want to. Now that the marriage has taken place, the friends of the girl have forsaken her, and they claim they will have nothing further to do with her.

For the time being, the young couple will reside with Mrs. Franking's parents. Mr. Franking will keep on with his studies in the law department, but Mrs. Franking is undecided as to whether she will or not. It is thought by her friends, she intends to wait and see how she is received by the other coeds. Franking is reputed to be wealthy, and to the minister who married them, he said he was a Christian.

Tiam Hock Franking is a graduate of the Grand Rapids High school, having been a member of the class [of] 1910. While in the high school Mr. Franking was a prominent member of the High School House of Representatives, and distinguished himself in a number of oratorical contests. Principal Jesse B. Davis speaks highly of the young Chinese student, declaring that he was unusually bright, especially in the public speaking work.

He gave his reasons for leaving the Ann Arbor school and coming to the Grand Rapids high school, that he had heard that this city's school was the best in the state.

From the **Detroit Free Press,** *13 September 1912:*

ANN ARBOR GIRL WEDS CHINAMAN; BOTH STUDENTS

University City Stirred Up Over interracial Marriage of the Graduates.

EFFORTS OF PARENTS AND FRIENDS TO STOP IT VAIN

Intimates of Bride Now Declare They Will Have Nothing More to Do With Her.

Special to The Free Press.

Ann Arbor, Mich., September 13.—This whole town is agog over a wedding that occurred last Sunday, the news of which has just gotten out. The marriage was that of a Chinese student in the University of Michigan and an American girl, also a student in the university.

The marriage took place at the home of the bride's parents in this city, and Rev. W. O. Raymond, curate of the Episcopal church, performed the ceremony.

The bride is Miss Mae Watkins, a 1915 literary student, and the man she married, Tiam Franking, of Amoy, China, a junior law and one of the law debaters.

Cupid's Path Not Rose-Strewn.

The marriage was the culmination of a romance that started several years ago, when Franking first came to this country and entered the Ann Arbor High school, in which Miss Watkins was then a student. From then till now, the pathway of Cupid has been beset with all sorts of obstacles. At one time opposition on the part of Mr. and Mrs. Watkins was so great that it is said to have been the reason for Franking's leaving the city for a year. It is said that the parents were finally won over to the marriage rather than lose their daughter out of their lives.

Rev. Mr. Raymond tonight admitted that he had married the couple, but stated that before doing so he had questioned the father and mother of the bride, and that they had said to him, "Personality counts more with us than does race." After that Mr. Raymond no longer hesitated to marry the couple.

Bride's Friends Forsake Her.

The friends of the bride have tried for months to keep her from marrying the man, and have tried in every way to break off the friendship, but all to no avail. Even the stories of other Ann Arbor girls who had married foreign students were of no avail, for according to the bride she is never to be obliged to live in China, or in any foreign country, if she does not want to. Now that the marriage has taken place, the friends of the girl have forsaken her and assert they will have nothing further to do with her.

For the time being the young couple will reside with Mrs. Franking's parents. Mr. Franking will keep on with his studies in the law department, but Mrs. Franking is undecided as to whether she will or not. It is thought by her former friends that she intends to wait and see how she is received by the other co-eds. Franking is reputed to be wealthy, and to the minister who married them he said he was a Christian.

Tiam Franking is just now employed by a mercantile agency in Detroit, and has asked for authority to be transferred from the U. of M. to the Detroit College of Law in order that he may be nearer his business while finishing his law course.

From the **Detroit Free Press,**
14 September 1912:

CHINESE STUDENT
WEDS "M" GIRL

Parents and Friends Make Desperate Effort to Have Her Change Her Mind.

ANN ARBOR, Mich, Sept. 14.—Tiam Franking of Amoy, China, a junior law in the university, and Miss Mae Watkins, of this city, and a 1915 literary student, were married last Sunday by Rev. W. O. Raymond. Friends of the couple had kept the matter a secret.

The marriage was the culmination of a romance that started several years ago when Franking first entered Ann Arbor high school, in which Miss Watkins was a student. The parents and friends of the girl did everything possible in an effort to thwart the marriage. At one time the opposition made by Mr. and Mrs. Watkins was so great that it is said to be the cause of Franking leaving the university town for a year.

Girl friends of the bride, who tried in every way to have her give up Franking, have forsaken her.

Franking, who is working with a mercantile agency in Detroit, has asked the university authorities for a transfer to the Detroit College of Law. He states that he can keep his present position and also go on with his law course.

Miss Watkins has not decided whether she will finish her course or not.

Letter to the Editor, Ann Arbor Times:

COMMUNICATION

To the Editor:

I would be more than pleased and grateful to have my name occupy the space in the Ann Arbor Times, if it were not for the fact that some of the statements appeared, are untrue and unsound. Consequently to support the great American source of information, that must or ought to represent the public fairly and justly and at the same time to give the public a correct and unprejudicial news, this article is deemed advisable, if not necessary. From what source the newspaper reporters obtained their information, concerning such personal affairs, I know not, but as a citizen from China, the oldest country though the youngest republic; and as a law student in the United States of America, the youngest nation, though the oldest republic, I consider it my duty to assist in explaining away some of the erroneous publications, where truth and justice can be easily secured. Therefore, let it be the aim and duty as well of our American friends to exercise due care and prudence in obtaining information that would in some degrees involve personal character and personal reputation. Let the publication be actual and accurate, and not be sensational.

For proof there is neither time nor space to be wasted here to show the falsity of some of the statements in question. However, few points may be well and briefly raised here.

Do the people know when my acquaintanceship started, so as to affect my change from the engineering to law course and from the Ann Arbor high school to Grand Rapids high school?

Are the people aware of this fact, that from the very first day I knew the family, I never had received a word or an act of unpleasant feeling?

Do not her classmates both in the Ann Arbor high school and in the University of Michigan know what kind of student she is?

Don't the marriage confirmed with laws of both holy gospel and the land, and with the consent of the parents, as well as the parties—to the understanding and appreciating the life and happiness embodied in those simple words, "Ideal Home," after all a private matter?

What more do people expect except to love on right principle, and to become true husband and wife?

To do justice and fair play, I shall be more than ready and pleased to render satisfactory reasons and proof for accusing the unfounded and unauthorized publication and information. I shall not be busy this week—my place at Detroit is Room 203, 'The Abbey,' both phones, 1954.

May I hope in closing that the people of these two republics will have a chance to know and understand each other better than in the past; and the friendship of these two nations may be made warmer and closer in the future, through the exchange of ideas and ideals of the present.

Am deeply indebted under whose hands this is published.

TIAM H. FRANKING.
Sept. 15, 1912.

Oct. 12, 1912

Dearest Mae,—

. . . . This place [Oriental Café, 63 Michigan Avenue, Detroit] will perhaps open on Saturday, but with great certainty—will on Monday. . . .

My class work is alright now—I have one or two fellows told me so—that I hit the nail at the right place. I made pretty good recitations now & in fact good start with every professor that I am having. Two or three fellows talk with me about my plan to practice here & they all asked me about "that point," citizenship. They told me to be up on that question. . . .

Remember me to them most kindly, & accept my love,

I am,
your Tiam

Ann Arbor, Mich.
January 6, 1913
Monday afternoon

Dear Tiam

We have the nicest little grand-son here you ever saw. Born about half past one this P.M. Is an old bouncer as we say when we mean a good sized child. From present glimpses I think he looks like his papa. Hope you can come soon to see him. Mae got through finely and is resting nicely now. Write soon.

Lovingly—
Mother

6/19/13; 11 P.M.

Dearest,—

The degree title of Bachelor of Law is now mine—it [is] vested in me for all time. Tho you were not there, I am however thankful for the applause—In fact—I received the most of them all! Of course—I did not expect anything but that diploma tonight, but my surprise, there were pretty bouquets waiting for me— some of them with addresses on & some I could not find any. Anyway to let you share my joys & cheers of this occasion, I am sending some of the nicest flowers. . . .

Your,
Tiam

East Northfield,
Massachusetts
6/25/13

Dearest Mae,—

At last—your letters reached me last evening here at the conference Post office. . . .

I am expecting Mr. Brockman to be here very soon. After that I hope I shall be in a position to know just where & what I shall be & do in China.

Very likely along the Christian work—for that seems to be the most urgent & important of all the callings, as expressed in various speeches and discussions. Even among men who were different government positions & educational work still they selected the Y.M.C.A. work. The reason for this is that China is facing a second revolution—A revolution of the heart. . . .

Remember me to all.
Your
Tiam

Home
December 16, 1913

My own dearest Tiam,—

And so this is the day you sail! There is an added ache in my heart at the thot; just why, I hardly know, (unless it is because you will be farther away from me, physically, for a little while). For I realize, Dear, that the sooner you go, the sooner baby and I may be with you again; and I know, too, that I am entrusting my Beloved Boy, not to the mercy of the irresponsible ocean, but to the mercy of the boundless love of God. He brot you to me once, halfway round the world, and now he will guide me to you again; for He meant, I believe, that our lives should be one. So, in spite of the ache, there is comfort in my heart and hope.

Your letter of December 13 reached me on the first mail delivery this morning. Dearest, I am glad you did not send me anything more for my birthday or Christmas than your letters with their messages of love and remembrance. Those messages, my darling, are more precious far to me than all the gifts money could buy. The love and trust of my husband is a perpetual gift. . . . Nelson is so dear and funny now, and does so many cute things. . . . You remember how he liked to turn off and on the light, and knew where all the switches were even before you left. Dad still carries him around at night to turn them off and on. Several evenings ago, he took him out on the back porch and showed him the moon. It was almost full and really looked very much like the light in the store. Nelson looked at it a moment, then turned and fumbled around with his hand until he found *something to turn. It was a clothespin on the line . . . he twisted it, then looked to see if the moon had "gone out." . . . And now I must close but first, let me say again to put aside all doubts and worries; soon we will be together again, and always. I am your own faithful and devoted wife.*

Love and kisses from
Nelson and Mae

S. S. Tenyo Maru
No. 221
Jan 1st, 1914

Dearest Mae,—

. . . . *To begin with, my stay about 8 or 9 hours in Honolulu was a pleasant one. It was in fact . . . delightful to view such a beautiful tropical place. . . . I mailed you my letter that cost me 12 cents, and I spent 10 cents for 1 ice cream soda, & 10 cents for orange & 10 cents for Chinese dish. . . .*

So much for the happy side of the journey—let me tell you just a little of the darkness on the voyage. A child . . . died after 5 or 6 days journey. He was about 21 months old & sick. . . . There is one or two passengers who have been seasick pretty hard. . . . This leads me to write you that when you come with our baby you must take special good care in your journey. . . . When the time comes for you to take such trip, I shall write & send you a guide or direction of my own telling you just how to start your trip & spend your time & money & where. . . .

With love & kisses
Tiam

Association Bldg.
120 Szechuen Rd.
Shanghai, China
Feb. 5, 1914

Dearest Mae,—

. . . . *Well, school opens on Feb 6, (Fri). . . . Sometimes I was invited to join the party of high class (best recognized & most well known citizens of Shanghai) men, & other times I am looked down upon, because I am not their equal. However, my name in Shanghai is already bigger than myself.*

I wrote you about your coming, & I hope I can send you the money as I wrote. . . . But don't be afraid because you are going to travel alone. Be yourself & use your common sense & generous spirit; perhaps things will be more pleasant for you than other wise. The money in America counts a great deal especially when compared with here. According to the present exchange $1—in USA will *[be] worth about $2.10 here, hence 1 cent saved there, it will bring you 20 cashes here, which is enough for the poor people in China to live in one day.*

I have not felt well since my return. Shanghai is pretty cold. So don't think it is a warm place & that you will leave your winter dresses. You need pretty near everything you had in America. . . . Bring your guitar (there is a demand of music in Shanghai, especially of women). If you don't teach in school, you will have plenty of time to amuse yourself with music. If you want to teach, I think we can arrange somehow when you come. This, as you will see, will mean that your Latin & German & English education will hold good in China, if you wish to use them. . . . The glee club made up of men & women impressed upon me more & more that you must not let the Chinese women beat you. Especially they all asked me can Mrs. F. play or sing. . . . Anyhow it matters not whether you can or not so long as you are the right kind of wife to me.

Today, I have been figuring a little that my present income will cover our expenses when you come with a surplus of about $30—each month. The $70 or more of course includes two houses & one servant.

In the mean time when I have opportunity, I shall commence to find one more job so that our income will at least be $200—a month & we must have that much in order to live reasonably & fairly in Shanghai. . . .

With love & kiss to you & baby & best regards to all your Tiam

> *120 Szechuen Rd.*
> *Shanghai, China*
> *Feb. 12th, 1914 (Holiday in China)*

Dearest Mae,—

Today I received two of your letters—one including a letter from my brother who told me that my parents are thinking of me all the time. . . .

I have all together 15 hours work a week. 5 days & half weekly. Six subjects in all some 1 hour others 2 & others 3 or 4 hours a week. They are all easy & interesting, such as [modern & Roman history] Shakespeare on English (Literature & Reading) composition & advanced geography. In order to get ahead of the students, I am reading the Mid-Summer Night's Dream for Lang. Lit, & Tempest for Reading. . . .

I am waiting till you come before I get everything for our home. I am in other words some what neglecting myself here. But I have no complaint to make since my return, tho there are many times when I have to adjust myself & swallow big stone in order to suit the conditions of the place. I feel it is only fair to you to make this long journey of yours early to China where you have a rightful house awaiting you. . . .

With love & kisses to you & baby Your Tiam

120 Szechuen Rd.
Shanghai, China
Feb. 22, 1914

Dearest Mae,—

I am now writing to let you know that I have started my work in teaching beautifully. I am teaching only the higher classes, ie. 6th, 5th, & 1 class in 4th class. They understand the English language pretty well, but they want to know everything in the books, so you can see how I am situated. . . .

Since I came to Shanghai, my name I guess has been on the magazine or pamphlets & papers. Some time I discovered it too late, & other time they use only my Chinese name in Chinese, so I did not attempt to send you any. . . .

I have a petition already written to the government at Peking for a license to practice law as soon as I can find one who is giving up there. I am planning to do some law work if I can later, if not I want to be admitted to the courts here any how. And I think I can find a partner later on. . . .

I hope I can send you the $100—gold in about 2 weeks now. I trust that you will be ready upon receiving my money to leave for your husband. . . .

I received a letter from my mother in answer to my letter to her. She still expressed that I disobeyed my father, but she asked me to go home at least a week or two. She also asked whether you are here in Shanghai or not. From the tone of her letter, I can make up with [her] easily, but she has to do what my father thinks or regards the matter. Even that I have no fear to overcome my father & those who laughed at me now. Because I have been a very mischievous boy. "Am I?" I guess so. . . .

So far I have been going to the Free Christian Church the sermon in English that is why I went.

> *With love & kiss to you & baby*
> *your Tiam*

Remember me to all & that I am
thinking all of them constantly

"Home"
April 28, 1914
10:00 A.M.

My own dearest Tiam,—

. . . . First, however, I have something definite to tell you, dear, at last—our date of departure. We will sail from Vancouver on June 25 on the "Empress of India", and reach China July 14. I hope, Tiam dear, that you will think it all

right for me to change the route you directed. Surely anything is better than to wait until the Tenyo Maru sails in August, don't you think?

Mama, Nelson & I went to the M.C. station last Thursday to see about the Pacific mail steamers. Their rates are the same as the T.K.K. but they all go to Hong Kong & Philippines first, and make such long stops at different ports that it takes about a month and half to reach Shanghai. So the ticket agent suggested the Canadian Pacific Mail steamers (Empress Ships). They go direct across from Vancouver to Japan then to Shanghai—shortest route & fastest time. He couldn't find the 2nd class rates listed but the first class were the same as the T.K.K. steamers, and the sailing of June 25 seemed very satisfactory. He made out several R.R. routes across the continent, and we came home to discuss & think it over. . . . (Dearest, I am so excited about your letter and the new house and going and everything I can't write straight. Please pardon it this time.) . . . I saw several advertisements . . . for the Great Northern S.S. Co. sailing direct from Seattle. That would have been a good route as I could go from Chicago to Seattle direct . . . 2nd class on the G.N.S.S. however is $115 & 3rd class is $85, so I gave up that idea. . . . He called up the general agent of the Canadian Pacific. The agent said . . . those ships were for benefit of Asiatic travellers only. However, he explained to him about me, and that I took your nationality, so the man thot it would be alright. . . . Yesterday (Monday) morning he called me and said they had reserved cabin 303 for me, and would send the ticket, also some baggage markers so that my baggage can be checked from Ann Arbor straight thru to Shanghai, and I won't have to attend to it at Vancouver. . . . So, dearest, it is all settled, and we will be together quite soon after all. Tho, I wish we were there already, I do want my Boy so much. I want you, dearest Tiam, and I want to help you with everything—your home and your work,—yourself. If I did not have so many things to do in getting ready, I would never be able to wait for the time to come; but as it is I will have every moment occupied, with sewing and packing & general preparations, besides some time that I am spending in finishing up the picture contest. [Mae entered Nelson in a baby contest, and he won first place.]

Dearest, are you disappointed that I will not be there as early as you first planned? Believe this, dearest, you do not want me or need me one bit more than I want and need my own precious Boy. Our separation more than two-thirds gone already. Be patient, Tiam dear, and take good care of yourself. Don't work too hard, dear, take plenty of rest and recreation of the safe, right kind. Sweetheart, you know what I mean. I trust you, darling, only I want to be sure you are safe. Every moment you are in my thots.

But about the route I will take across the continent: I can go from Chicago to Seattle, then by small boat to Victoria or Vancouver. (The ship takes on passengers at both those places in starting as they are only a few miles apart.) Or I can go by rail from Seattle to Vancouver. Or I can go from Chicago to St. Paul and there take a through sleeper to the coast. Just at present that line runs tourist sleepers (the kind I will take) to Seattle, and Standard sleepers (higher-priced) to Vancouver. But I could change at Mission, first before I get to Vancouver, and ride in a day coach to Vancouver at noon. However, the agent said that travel would be heavier by June, and very likely they would run tourist cars to Vancouver. In that case, that will be the route for me to take. It will, incidentally, be a little cheaper than the other—about $59.75. (The fare to Frisco will be higher by June, too, but of course that won't affect me). I am sure your instructions will be just as helpful, even if I am going a different way, and I shall read again and carry them with me, dear. . . .

> Love & best wishes as ever, with love and kisses from Nelson & me
> As ever your own faithful & devoted wife,
> Mae

> "Home" until June 19th
> May 3, 1914 Sunday Evening

My own dearest Tiam,—

. . . . This afternoon we all went for a walk (except Gwen, who had made a previous date with Lucille) on the way home, Mama and I stopped at Webbs for some soda. . . . They had those Chinese lanterns on the lights, and it reminded me of the first time that we went there. You said "The lantern over your head is different from all the rest." And so it was, for it was a sort of diamond-shaped one, while the others were round or oval. I looked for it today, but it was not among the rest. Dearest Tiam, I wonder if you know how full of memories of my Boy this town is to me? Everywhere I go, there is a street where we have walked together, or a building where we have been. Today, in passing the Hill Memorial building, we saw, thru the upper windows, the collection of Musical instruments, that had been transferred from the campus. And I thot of the time I first saw them,—when we went to the Museum that afternoon almost five years ago. Oh, Tiam darling, I cannot find any words to express the love and longing for you that is in my heart. Last night I dreamed that I was on a ship going to you. I seemed to be standing by the rail, looking over at the water, and I was thinking that every moment I was coming nearer to you. The thot made me so glad—so intensely happy that I began to cry. And I woke from my dream actually crying.

I suppose you have moved, by this time, into the new house that is to be our home,—Our Home, dearest. Oh, I am so anxious to see it all, so interested in everything you write about. But most of all, of course, it is My Boy I want to see.

*The rest, tho important, is only secondary. For I should be happy to go anywhere—
north, south, east or west, so long as I go to my husband. . . .*

    *I am so glad, dearest, that your mother urges you to come home for a visit. She
must be so anxious to see her son—who was once the dear baby boy for whom
"she used to reach things that he could not reach." But Tiam, even she,—your
Mother, from who you have been separated for years, cannot yearn to see you with
the intensity of longing which I feel.—I, your wife, who have been separated from
you for only a few months. It is often claimed that Mother-love is the most powerful,
the most wonderful, in the universe. But I believe firmly that the love of a true
wife is more powerful, more wonderful than the other. A true woman will suffer,
will sacrifice for the sake of her child, but if that child is a true "pledge of love" as
children should be, then all the suffering, all the sacrifice, are primarily for the
sake of the man who is the father of her child, and the love of a wife has all the
protective qualities of the love of a Mother with many more—deeper, truer, more
intimately tender than Mother-love can ever know. Children grow up and form
new ties, while parents grow aged and pass into the world beyond. But husband
and wife walk together, side by side, hand in hand,—as you and I shall walk,
dearest,—as you and I must walk because we love each other.*

    *So long as you are my husband, all mine, and mine alone, I shall be happy,
dearest. For just to be with you, dearest, secure in the knowledge that our love is
true and faithful, is happiness to me. Often in the night I recall the feeling of rest
and contentment that was mine, just to lie beside you and know that we loved each
other. And in my loneliness now, it is a great comfort to recall that restful, happy
time; but, dearest, it is an even greater comfort to look forward to the time when I
shall again be beside you, with no thot of coming separation to make me sad. Oh,
Tiam sweetheart, these memories and these hopes are my very life. . . .*

                        *With lots of love and kisses from Baby and me,
                        and Love from Mother and Daddy.
                        As ever,
                        your Mae*

                                    *The Strand Hotel
                                    Vancouver, B.C.
                                    [n.d.]*

Dear Mama, Dad & Gwen,—

    *Nelson did very nicely until we reached Chicago and made the transfer to the
Soo line station. . . .*

    *There were lots of nice people in our coach & we all enjoyed the entire trip as
much as possible. It was cold & rainy when we left Chicago, & indeed there was
never a moment when we were too warm. . . . Part of Saturday & all day Sunday*

we were crossing the prairies. I was interested in them at first but they soon grew monotonous & I couldn't get Nelson to look out of the window at all. . . .

We entered the mountains Monday morning early, & the rest of the trip was one grand feast of scenery. Nelson enjoyed it too, & looked out of the window with as much rapture and absorption as the oldest traveller. . . . The mountains themselves were beautiful beyond my expectations. They are not at all like the postcards would have one believe, tho. There is nothing gaudy about their colorings. But I can't describe them now, I'm too sleepy. I hope you are not too lonesome. Of course I would like to see you all & I miss you, but I cannot help being very happy & glad to be going to Tiam. . . .

Lovingly, Mae

Canadian Pacific Railway Co.
R.M.S. "Empress of India"
Sunday, July 5, 1914

Dearest Mother, Dad & Gwen,—

. . . . Well, we are "old and seasoned travellers" now,—the baby and I, tho I am too anxious to get to Shanghai to enjoy the trip very much—"I want to see Tiam."

. . . . So here we are, Mother dear . . . going all the way across the continent of North America, and the Pacific ocean—in one suit case and a lunch basket, so to speak. By the way this silk waist is going to pieces, I begin to think that I shall have to get off at Shanghai with nothing on but the lunch basket. What shall I do if the wind blows that off?

. . . . I was very sick for the first four or five days. So I went & explained to the Purser, & the Captain had us transferred to a first class cabin, and we have all our meals served right in the room. (You needn't say "ha, ha," yet. Mama, It's too early, you know.) Nelson is happy and contented with me. He says "there it goes" (when he drops anything). . . . I wish you were all here, going with us. I think every day how Dad would enjoy the meals, he could fish every day and three times a day at that.

. . . . We are due at Yokohama in a day or two now, and a week from tomorrow should arrive at Shanghai. It seems long to wait. It seems ages & ages since I left you all in Ann Arbor. I hope you are getting over the lonesome part more, and beginning to have a good time during the summer vacation. Just be hopeful, Mother dearest, as you always must be—and almost always are. Of course you will have moments, perhaps days, of discouragement. But remember at the time that they are only temporary. The months will pass, as the days are doing now, and soon we shall all be together again, please God.

You must know that I miss you all, and wish so much that you were with me now. Yet you must also be glad—as I am glad—that I love My Boy enough to be happy to go to him with no thot of turning back. Because I have to go to my husband, anyhow, and it would be sad indeed if I went unwillingly or regretfully. He deserves all the love, sympathy and help that I can bring to him, and I want him to have it. I know you realize this as well as I, and it is a comfort to me to know that too. . . . Good bye dear, kiss Dad & Gwen for baby Nelson & me, they can kiss you back for the same. We're still chums in spirit aren't we mutterchen?

Your own loving daughter,
Mae

Shanghai, China
July 24, 1914

Dearest Mother, Dad & Gwen,—

I have been looking for a letter from you for several days, as I suppose you wrote me here soon after I left. But no doubt it hasn't had time to arrive yet. How are you all getting along this warm weather? Had any picnics on the island yet?

Nelson is playing here in the room with Tiam as I write this. He has on his shirt and "ponts." Nothing more, altho today is cooler than we have had in some time. July and August are the hot months in this part of China, and they say it is hotter than usual this year. I don't think it is a much higher temperature than that week in June before we left Ann Arbor, only it continues for more days at a time. However I was expecting even hotter weather, as the stewardess on the steamer told me it was very bad at this time of year here. It was cold all the way across the Pacific, and then when we reached Japan it became warm suddenly and each succeeding port was hotter than the last.

Finally at Nagasaki the pilot for Shanghai got on, and told Miss Morgan (the stewardess) who was with me on deck at the time that they were having hotter weather at Shanghai than there. So I was prepared for it, and compared with my expectations, the reality seemed almost cold. . . . Nelson . . . is keeping well and is happy most of time, altho he won't let me out of his sight for a moment, and insists on my carrying or holding him every time we go anywhere. We haven't done much walking as there are all sorts of conveyances here,—automobiles, carriages, street cars (they call them trams here, the same as in Canada & England) and ricshas. I enjoy the last-mentioned best, perhaps because they are more of a novelty to me, but they are very "springy" and easy to ride in. The tram cars are much like ours there except they are divided into two parts 1st & 3rd class. We have been "shopping" several times, so I have seen something of the business places here. They have large department stores in which you might almost forget you were in

China (only I don't want to forget it). Tiam bot me a very pretty white waist &
skirt and undershirt last week. (My baggage won't be here until next month.)

We have made several calls and been entertained at dinner & at tea; have also
received visitors and entertained at dinner. Everyone is very nice to me. So you see
I am having a good time. You ought to see the babies. The streets are full of the
dearest, funniest little ones,—some in Chinese dress, some in American, some in
Japanese, and few in no dress at all. We met the cutest little girl about three years
old and named Lucille. Her sister's name is Laura.

Tiam had the house all arranged when we came. You know he understands such
things very well and we have added some things since then. I wish you could see it,
and no doubt you will some day. It is just a nice size to be comfortable and we
have matting on all the floors. Don't you envy us? We have a good maid too, so I
don't need to do any work except a little general supervision. But I have been
having lots of fun trying to bake without any cook books. Have made plain biscuits
& cinnamon rolls, layer cake, Chinese cakes with cinnamon in place of the
almonds, and custard. We use Borden's Eagle Brand Condensed milk. Had some
welsh rarebit last night, but no bad dreams. I am going to try some pie soon. . . .

I cannot give you much definite information yet in regard to business. But Tiam
thinks you ought to do very well with a bakery here. I noticed several foreigners
including a Scotch bakery. They look very clean and prosperous and they charge
enormously. But there are lots of foreigners to buy the goods. The population in
Shanghai is about 500,000, and so I think you could easily find an opening. Rents
are comparatively high just now, as many people came here from the interior during
the revolutionary disturbances. There is lots of building going on in both residence
and business sections. Of course the imported canned & bottled goods are very
expensive as you have to pay the American price plus the cost of importation plus
the dealer's profit. And one can buy almost anything of American manufacture. I
don't see why you couldn't make money baking. Fresh milk is about the same as
there, also sugar & baking powder. But no doubt you could get wholesale prices.
Lard is high, but that is the imported—Swift's compounds etc. Tiam says the
Chinese get the meat & try out their own lard. That of course would make it very
cheap, and no doubt you could arrange it on a practical basis. We are buying eggs
now at ten cents per dozen. There must be lots of money in ice cream with eggs,
milk & ice so reasonable, they charge 25 cents for a dish about two-thirds the size
of our 5 cent dishes!! You had better bring your own kitchen utensils of all kinds,
as it is hard to find just what you want here. And I think it would be cheaper to
bring what you already have. You see you could get all the cleaning, dishwashing
etc. done very cheaply, and give your whole attention to the baking where you would
get the biggest returns for your work. Will give you more information concerning
things as we learn more definitely ourselves.

From present indications, I shall be able to find some teaching to do, without difficulty, and as that will be of advantage to us in every way—particularly just now—I do not want to let the opportunity pass.

I don't think I mentioned this in my last letter to you, as I wrote very hurriedly, but the first thing I noticed upon my arrival was that My Boy had a very persistent cough. He says he has had it ever since he came here. I was awfully worried about it, as I was afraid it might be tubercular. A lady who called on us a few days ago—she teaches in the Y.M.C.A, too and has a doctor's degree—was speaking about it, and she said the safe way would be an examination, but she thot it sounded more like chronic bronchitis than a tubercular cough. I had already given him my inhaler to use and it helped him very noticeably at once. However, we have been unable to get the hyonier [inhaler] at any of the drug stores here. One man said they had it here about twelve years ago, but he didn't think it could be found anywhere in the city now. So could you send us a bottle by parcel post? And a piece of gauze if you have any extra ones. We got a jar of mentholatum, and have been rubbing that on the outside. It helps some, but is nothing like so effective as the hyonier.

Is that helmet of Tiam's there all right yet? They wear them a lot here, and they are about $4.00. That one was new and all right; and you could send it by parcel post for just a few cents.

When you have time, take the cook book of mine with the oil cloth covers and write the recipe for sponge cake, molasses cake or that ginger bread, white bread, plum pudding, & spice cake. Use measures instead of weights. And I'd like one of those . . . cookbooks, also a John Dough one. Want a lot of things, don't I, Mama dee? And if you have a chance, you might get me those knives & forks of grandma's that Aunt Nora said she was keeping for me. They cost so much here that it would not be practical to buy them, as we have Chinese cooking most of the time, and chopsticks are better for that. We have the prettiest red chop-sticks! Nelson generally has to hold them, if he can't eat with them. He wants to do everything he sees either of us doing. If Tiam coughs, then he coughs too. If I reach up to arrange a picture on the wall he insists on going thru the same motions. . . .

> *With love from us all, and a kiss*
> *from Nelson for Mama, Dad & Gwen*
> *Mae & Tiam*

P.S. I gave you Tiam's business address Y.M.C.A. Our residence is in a new part. Chinese name, so the address in English is a little uncertain yet. But try this address in your next letter or card—Mrs. T.H. Franking, 39 Fu Teh Lee, North Szechuen Road, Shanghai, China.

39 Fu Teh Li,
N. Szechuen Road
Nov. 18, 1914

Dearest Mother, Dad & Gwen,—

. . . . Dear me! from what I read in the paper about the war's effect on prices in America it seems to me that everything you use is going up—sugar, spices, nutmeats and everything. Tiam has written to some Chinese in America who he helped to go there in the securing of passports—to send you fifty dollars gold and we can pay it here when the exchange is more favorable. If you do not get it within two or three months from this writing let us know and we will send it at once. . . .

Hope business will be better. Everybody feels the effect of the war, I guess. But don't blame the Kaiser. He has got six sons on the firing line and I don't think he likes it any better than anybody else. But I will send you a news clipping, which will give you a clearer idea of the true situation—if you read it carefully—than I can. England makes me sick—parading before the world her "virtuous indignation" over Germany's violation of Belgium's neutrality and pretending she is fighting to avenge that crime, while on the other hand she aids her ally Japan in violating China's neutrality in capturing Tsingtan—the German fortified city on the China coast. England is simply fighting to smash Germany because she is jealous of the "made in Germany" articles, while Germany has got to fight to keep herself on the map in the face of Russian aggression. Lovely weather we've been having, isn't it?

. . . . We see some very funny items concerning the war. For example there was one today about a German soldier who captured twelve French soldiers. He made them all write their names on a post card, which he then sent home to his wife. Some days ago, I was reading that the recruiting in England went very slowly at first owing to the antiquated methods and needless restrictions which were all right in peaceful times but should have been cast aside in such an emergency. It took three weeks to get 100,000 men which could be recruited in New York & Chicago in "twenty-four" hours. One man protested in a letter to the paper. This is what he wrote:

"I want to go to the front and fight. They won't have me because some of my teeth are bad. D——n it! I don't want to bite the Germans; I want to shoot them."

Well goodbye
Love & "best kisses" as Gwen wrote from us all.

39 Fu Teh Li
N. Szechuen Road
Shanghai, China
December 14, 1914

Dearest Mother, Dad and Gwen:

. . . . Am glad you like the Church of Christ. The older I get and the more I
see and hear, the more I believe that we should get away from Christianity and
doctrine and creeds, and find Christ. It seems to me that Christianity at present is
very far away from Him, tho nearer than it was during the last century.

We laughed about Tiam's overcoat going to the Belgians. I don't know why. If it
can keep somebody warm that will be a cause for thankfulness. But I don't see
anything funny in Mrs. Weidman sending things to them. . . .

Mind you, this is no Eulogy of Germany . . . I am not canonizing them all as a
Nation of Saints. She has her good and her bad, her ambitions and her greed as
every nation has (even England. I grant that much). But she also has a right to
make herself as prosperous and commercially great as the industry and frugality
of her people will permit. That is what England denies her. That is the foundation
stone upon which this hideous structure of ruin and devastation and slaughter has
been reared. (And I learned that in history at the University of Michigan.) Tho I
did not, could not, learn to what lengths England's insatiable demands to be and
remain mistress of the sea as in every sense would lead her. I doubt if any one at
that time could have conceived it. England hasn't got to crush Germany in order to
preserve civilization. Secretly she knows it, but she thinks she has to crush her in
order that she herself may remain supreme. And she is going to get the same
notion in regard to the United States when that nation proceeds to fulfill her
destiny commercially. Let me tell you a crushed and humiliated Germany will be a
far greater menace to the peace of the world than a Germany left to pursue her
legitimate way in peace and good will and where will be the gain to civilization
when Russia, barbarous in the truer sense of the word spreads herself like "an
ulcer which leechcraft may not cure," over the whole of Europe? Oh, you know to
the minutest detail, no doubt, of all the Belgians have suffered. Do you know what
the poor people of southern China have borne under the scourge of the Japanese
invaders? I think not—not if England has been able to prevent it—because Japan
is England's ally, her "dear little Brown brother" who shall fill his precious fists
with the coveted soil of China in spite of China's neutrality, in spite of her indignant
protests, when, helpless with the peril of fresh revolution at home she dare not do
more than protest. Is China's neutrality less sacred than that of Belgium? Are the
sufferings of China's people easier to bear or less to be pitied by the world at large
cause they were inflicted by England's ally instead of her enemy? Perhaps the fact

that they are added to the unspeakable crime of the opium curse with which England has fettered so many, body and soul, may aid in answering. . . .
Dec. 15
P.S. Tiam read my letter (he always does of course) and said I shouldn't tell you so much about what you don't know or you would think I was getting awfully big feeling here. I told him I thot I had made the point clear enough but would add a post script to be sure. . . .

What I despise about it is the self-righteous attitude of England and her deceit in placing the whole blame on Germany. Of course, Germany is partly to blame. If she hadn't backed Austria up the latter wouldn't have dared make such demands on Serbia. On the other hand, if Germany had known that England had a secret agreement with France and Russia binding her to fight with them if attacked, Germany would probably not have begun the war now. She did offer England every inducement—she promised to leave France in Europe intact and Belgium undisturbed. If England could keep out. But England was aching to fight and crush the commercial power of Germany. England didn't dare give the full facts to her people, so she has ranted and raved about the crime against Belgium and sent her army over—not to protect Belgium, for they haven't done it—but to protect her own pig-headed belief that she has got to "rule the waves." It isn't because I love Germany so much—tho I do admire and respect her. It is because I hate England with more bitterness than I ever felt before for her crimes against China and her pretended horror at what Germany has done that I cannot bear to have you give her credit which she doesn't deserve, and blame Germany for deeds more directly due to England. So far as concerns the men in the ranks and wives and Mothers and children they have left at home, I have as much sympathy for the suffering of one as another. But when it comes to the governments and the morals and principles involved, I believe that Germany is the only one with a shred of justification for fighting. Whatever motives led her into the war in the beginning she now is fighting for her very existence, and none of the others are at that necessity. By the time this reaches you, you will long have known most of what I am writing—in fact, some of the things I have said were also published in the Posts you sent me, but I don't think you have paid much attention to them. So now, having unburdened my mind and told you just where I stand and why, I will drop the subject with a "dull thud" and let it lie where it falls. Because otherwise it will take up more space than it should in my letters.

I made a mistake in the name of the place where Tiam is going to teach. It is a "National Institute" or something like that.

Dec. 16

. . . . From all of which, you will see that this "social ostracism" gets on my nerves,—or rather the absence of it, keeps me so continually on the move that I just have to stop and get some breath occasionally. I ought to be out making calls this minute. . . . Anyhow you know what I mean: your letter is more important than calls. . . .

You don't seem very far away from me. Sometimes you seem so near I can almost squeeze you. I hope you feel the same way. I will try to write to Aunt Louise. But I just don't get letters written to anybody except you. . . .

Love from Tiam, Mae, & Nelson

Shanghai
January 15, 1915

Dearest Mother, Dad & Gwen,—

. . . . [Nelson] is a comical little Bug. Wednesday evening as we were riding home on the street car the electric lights went out for a second or two. As soon as they got them on again Nelson looked around at me and laughed and said "Peek aboo lights."

. . . . I am having a "splendiferous" time teaching. Another case of the "old war-Horse" I guess. I begin to feel quite intelligent again and as tho I amounted to something, now that I no longer have to "pretend" that I am busy. Of course I have to neglect my calls and a few things that formerly took all my time, but somehow I feel as tho I were "getting somewhere."

Am also reviving another old ambition! I want a parrot. They have the darlingest fellow at the school. . . .

You'd die laughing to see Nelson boss the servants. One day Tiam couldn't get home for dinner so Nelson and I were eating alone. They [servants] stood behind his chair and finally one teased the other and they got to laughing. He turned around with the most reprovingly stern expression and said "Sh! Sh!" Another time when they had carried away the dishes from the table the pepper and salt were still left. Nelson called the older one in a sharp commanding tone and when she came he handed her the salt shaker. He didn't say anything more but the look he gave her along with the salt was an hour's lecture in itself. They are very nice with him tho, and entertain him real well. . . .

Well, it is half past ten, and I am so tired I will have to stop, tho I hate to; for, like you, it seems as tho I were having a visit with you. . . .

How did Gwen like her locket?
Love & best wishes from all of us. More next time.
Tiam, Mae, & Nelson

Chi Sue School
Pao Shin Road
Shanghai, China
Jan. 21, 1915

Dearest Mother, Dad & Gwen,—

I have given my physical Geography class some questions to write on, and so will scratch you a few lines to get off on the steamer that leaves tomorrow. . . .

Tiam has been admitted to the Mixed Court of the International Settlement, and that gives him the right to practice in the U.S. courts for China and the other courts here. So he is getting ready to open an office here, and we think you will be very glad to hear about it. He will have to give up some of the teaching and has decided to keep the Y.M.C.A. work as that is the most satisfactory, everything considered. Plans are also being made to open a law college here for the study of Chinese law this coming fall, and he expects to have a share in that work, too, which will be better than the commercial work and also more in his line. . . . I thot I was busy before, but I know I am busy now. It's "a happy kind of busy" tho. I think you would like to teach school in China and I know you could do it, too. . . .

Lovingly yours
Tiam & Mae
and Nelson

April 15, 1915

Dearest Mother, Dad & Gwen,—

Your letter of March 15 and the magazines were waiting when I got home this noon, and it certainly is good to get a letter again—sixteen days since the last— so you see it is as hard to wait for a letter at this end of the line as at yours. . . . Of course I opened the magazines to get my lace collar. It is lovely, Mama dear— and full of love, too, I am sure . . . it is much nicer because you made it, of course.

I am writing this in school while my history class is writing an examination. Feel sorry for 'em?

. . . . We do hope things will be easier soon. But when I think of Europe's battle fields and hospitals and desolate homes it seems as tho the rest of us are in heaven. Heaven only knows how soon it may be changed into hell for China with Japan pursuing her present policy. Of course we in Shanghai have the safest place, but the whole population are stirred up as never before. You know if Japan is attacked by another, England will have to help her, but not if Japan begins the attack herself. So she is fairly aching to make China start a fight. . . .

Bushels of love & best thots & kisses,
Tiam, Mae, Nelson

Shanghai, China
May 3, 1915

Dearest Mother, Dad & Gwen,—

Your letter of Mar. 22, and Gwen's came last week, together with the pretty Easter cards.

I should have written much sooner, but have been extra busy, and Tiam is not very well. Two weeks ago tomorrow evening he had a very bad hemorrhage from his lungs, and had to stay in bed a couple of days, and of course he still has to be very careful. But thinks he must work hard—two schools: the National Institute at Woosung and the Government Institute of Technology out near Shanghai, and then his law work. It's too much. . . .

Of course I am pretty much worried all the time now. Tiam probably has tuberculosis, tho if he is careful and has proper treatment there is no reason why he shouldn't get over it soon. But it furnishes quite a problem, and nearly made me sick myself, only I can't afford to let it do that. . . . I am writing this while my algebra class works problems. My Botany class is here & my last morning class, so goodbye till I dispose of 'em. . . .

Now good bye till next time. Will write to Gwen later.

Love & best wishes, Tiam, Mae, Nelson

Tiam H. Franking
Attorney and Counsellor-at-Law
17 Nanking Road
289 Avenue Joffre, French Concession
Shanghai, China
Sept. 2, 1915

Dearest Mother, Dad & Gwen,—

. . . . I was going to write so many things that I don't know what to start in with. But you ask so often about Tiam's work that I guess I may take that first. I am encouraging him to put more emphasis on his teaching than on the legal. He has done enough of the latter to make himself known as a lawyer, so he has the benefit of that. But with his health in the shape it is, teaching is far easier & better for him. It means a settled, definite income, for one thing, while the law does not—especially in the present unsettled condition of the country. And its expenses are trivial when compared with the upkeep of a large office with rent, telephone & the staff of servants and assistants necessary if one depends on the law work alone. Then, there is the constant worry about the conduct of cases & their outcome, and the trouble in collecting fees here & there & all over. With teaching,

we know how much is coming in, where it is coming from & when, and there
is no uncertainty about the work. Moreover, Tiam has established an excellent
reputation as a teacher here, has been widely advertised thru the different schools
& colleges, and is now connected with one of the best institutions in China—
Nanyang University. It has a larger campus than Michigan & many fine buildings
with splendid equipment. We will send you a catalog.

Sept. 7, Tuesday

I didn't expect to be so long in finishing this letter, but I had to stop at this point
& go to bed as I had not been feeling well for a couple of days. Had the doctor
come on the next day, & she gave me two kinds of powders & told me to stay in
bed. So I have been in bed since last Thursday, but am hoping I can get up in two
days more at the most. (Mama, I will explain a little more fully in a post script
which you can read to yourself and then burn up.) . . .

Tiam went to his first classes yesterday & has some more today so his work has
really begun. He had an offer yesterday of some work in the National Institute at
Woosung . . . but I told him he couldn't think of accepting it, because he has to go
there by rail & miss his lunch half the time or eat a cold one on the train; and
that, I think, is chiefly what weakened his health last spring. He will have some
work in this new law college just opening, & I don't want him to take any more
outside work. . . . But now he has the opportunity to repair the damages so I hope
he will not try to do any extra work. The free hours in the morning he can use
partly for rest & partly for any legal work he cares to do. He has turned down a
good deal on account of his health.

We have a lovely home here—one in a terrace of seven. There is a fancy brick
wall with two pretty iron gates shutting us off from the street, and also more brick
wall shutting us in from the neighbors on either side. The walls are about the
height of an ordinary person. Inside we have a dear little patch of yard with grass,
a bush in one corner & small bamboo branches & palms at the other corners, &
rows of potted plants up both sides of the cement walk & steps & across the front
of the porch. The porch is a nice large one—a pleasant place for afternoon tea.
There are double doors with small fancy shaped panes of colored glass. . . . Most
everything here that isn't Chinese is English. . . . This room has a fireplace with
green tiling & we have some very nice brass accompaniments. . . . The mantel
piece is carved & ornamented, & , like the rest of the wood work is stained &
varnished a mahogany color. The walls are plain white with raised molding &
ceiling borders and with similar circles at the center, from which the electric lights
are suspended. In this room we have a suite of drawing room furniture with
mahogany colored frames and red satin upholstery with a flowered design. . . .
Back of this room is a rather large hall with a pretty stairway, and back of the hall

a good-sized kitchen opening into the usual wash rooms & then outside finally.

Upstairs at the first turning is a medium sized bedroom there up at the top a hall, a bathroom, and a large front room over the living room below. This also has a fireplace with blue tiling, and it opens out onto the front porch upstairs. This is as large as a small bedroom, and is really a room more than a porch. It has a railing with cement posts supporting it, but above the railing are four glass sections which open outward, and below the railing are four removable, tight-fitting, wooden sections. So that either half may be opened or closed independently of the other. It's a delightful place to sleep or sew or study or eat, for that matter. And there are shade trees out in front which are constantly stirred by a breeze. I'm especially in love, however, with a Chinese lantern which covers the electric porch light here (upstairs), not the paper kind like they string up on the campus, but the carved-wood-and pictured-glass-kind like those hanging in the museum—only this is a dear little baby one, about fifteen inches high. We have electricity in all the rooms—a beautiful brass chandelier in the front room downstairs, a three-branched one (that can be raised or lowered) upstairs & single lights in the halls & smaller rooms. And there! I forgot to say that we have a third-story back porch, reached by a short flight of stairs from the second-floor hall.

We sold a good deal of furniture that we didn't want since moving here including two sets of dining chairs & a bedroom suite of eight pieces (inlaid oak). That's English style for you—eight pieces of bedroom furniture besides the bed. . . .

> *Love and kisses from*
> *Tiam, Mae, &*
> *Nelson*

P.S. I suppose you may feel rather worried if you don't know just what was the cause of my sickness. It was some kind of bladder trouble,—a little inflammation or something like that from a cold, I guess. But it brot on some other pains that were pretty dangerous to anybody with my expectations. [Mae was expecting the birth of their second son.] Everything seems to be all right now, tho, only I will have to be more careful about going up & down the stairs & carrying Nelson. The little imp! Before I had this trouble, he always insisted on my carrying him both ways, & if I refused on coming up, for example, he would make a great effort to drag himself up a step or two and would groan & breathe hard all the while & say it hurt his stomach. Well, he put up such a good bluff, I believed him, but since I have had to stay in bed, he has gone up & down alone a dozen times a day without a word. So I guess it must have been a bluff or else strong imagination. He must be going to develop into an actor instead of a pugilist.

> *Lovingly,*
> *Mae*

289 Ave. Joffre
French Concession
Shanghai, China
December 20, 1915

Dearest Mother, Dad & Gwen,—

There seems to be time for one more letter—the last of 1915. . . . I got the Xmas box . . . but we kept it to open on Xmas morning . . . and we are enjoying every bit of it. . . .

Nelson was going thru all the motions of using a needle & thread. . . . He told me "I sew box for baby."

But I was going to tell you about my arrangements. I had planned to go to the Shanghai Native Hospital, which is in charge of a Chinese lady doctor who is a friend of ours. I had arranged to have Nelson with me too, with an amah, of course, to take care of him, only he would eat & sleep in the same room with me. I don't want to stay at home, because in addition to the fact that everything is more convenient at the hospital, I am afraid it would be very hard for Tiam to have so much confusion & excitement in the house. His hemorrhages always resulted from unusual excitement or confusion before and . . . I don't want to take any chances.

Well, on account of this attempt at a "third Revolution" it isn't safe for us to go to the hospital, which is unfortunately situated between the gun-boats on the water and the arsenal on the shore. However, Dr. Chang has made arrangements for us to go to her house, and so Tiam will take us over on Saturday afternoon—January 1, 1916, and the nurse will come there too. So I am pretty busy just now getting things straightened around here and packing suitcases & things. . . .

Now good bye for a little while. With love & best wishes as well as appreciative thanks from Tiam, Mae & Nelson

P.S. 1/4/16 A note from Dr. says to us a boy
                          Tiam
[Letter from Mae to Mr. and Mrs. Henry O. Watkins]
Enclosed were two birth notices:

Alason Franking
Newly arrived
extends
New Year's Greetings
Jan. 5, 1916   wt 8 lbs
Mr. & Mrs. Tiam H. Franking

289 Avenue Joffre
Shanghai, China
July 25, 1916

Dearest Mother, Dad, and Gwen,—

Your letter of June 20th received July 20th. It was the one about "June 19th. wrap-it-up-in lavender-and-old-lace", but the lavender atmosphere was considerable dispelled by George Fitch's feet.

Your "news" in regard to Mabel's marriage was certainly news to me all right. The last two letters she wrote I never got around to answer, for it was while Tiam was sick and before the baby came. So I haven't heard from her for over a year, tho I sent her one of the baby's birth cards. The stingy thing might at least have sent an announcement, but if she can't afford to tell me the name of the guy she married, you need not take the trouble to do so. What's the difference anyway, aren't we all "planks and driftwood"?

How is Nutty Dick at this writing? Still the "baddest"? We don't got no cat now whatever—nor no dog, nor nothing, except kids. Everything's unsanitary except kids, and sometimes I think they's a little unsanitary. But they are highly valuable and incidentally entertaining,—"queer pie but I like it" you know.

We have had some extremely hot weather—half way up the nineties, but the last few days are cooler again. Tiam is supposed to be having a vacation, but he has one law case on hand and is preparing a text book on English Composition for the college English classes. So I am afraid his vacation is "taking" itself far, far away? or else "in the sweet bye-and-bye". In this connection, you will notice that my thots are vacating to such an extent that I am obliged to substitute ready-made ones which are somewhat worn. Afraid I'll wear out the [ribbon] on the typewriter before I have done.

We had two telegrams from my Chinese mama lately, saying that she expects to come for her visit soon now. If you'd get that aeroplane out and come along too, we'd show you a good time. And you could hold the babies too. I called Nelson "baby" the other day, and then I said, "Are you a baby?" He said "No, I Nelson." And I asked, "But what are you" and he said "I three years old live in China." Yesterday he looked up at me and asked "Have you got Chinese eyes?" And when I told him "No," he said "I got Chinese eyes." But little near-curly-top doesn't intend to be any down-trodden worm. One day he was playing in his high-chair with an empty powder tin, when Nelson was suddenly seized with a desire to play with the same tin, and started to pick it up. Alason grasped the situation, like wise the tin with both hands, voiced an exceedingly emphatic protest and looked up to me for help, all at the same time. . . . Nelson got a tin somewhere else. Nothing slow about a man that could put up a triple line of defense like that "on the spur of the

moment" so to speak! I expect things will be superlatively exciting around here in
a year or two. . . .

Close with love . . . from the Franking family.

Per Mae

289 Ave. Joffre
Shanghai, China
September 19, 1916

Dearest Mother, Dad & Gwen,—

*. . . . My Chinese Mama has been here a week now, but I haven't had a chance
to write to you until now. All last week I was busy getting the book ready for
the publishers, and then I had about seventy compositions to correct which had
been waiting for me. That is out of the way now, and so I will take the time this
morning to write you a few lines. However, as I have a cold and cold sore and a
sore throat, you must not expect too much in the way of a letter.*

*My Chinese Mama—I suppose you are more interested in her than in my sore
throat etc. is just as nice as ever—or I might say, nicer, because this time I wasn't
scared of her at first. . . . She wants Nelson to go home with her for a few months
visit, and he may do so. In fact, she would be glad to take both of them "for
keeps." But of course that is out of the question. Tiam's brother came with her—
the one who was home from the Philippines to be married—and also her brother's
boy, who is going to stay here and go to school. And also a woman who is going
to stay with us as housekeeper, and her boy who will help here. Then there will
always be someone at the house whom we can depend on to look after the
servants, and the children, when we go away without them.*

*Merciful heavens! Don't say anything about anybody else's house. I don't know
what ours would look like if there wasn't somebody to do every hand's turn that is
done in it. . . .*

*There is a newspaper clipping inside. And how do you like the thot that all your
family news was perused by the British Authorities here—together with all the
other family and business news from America to China—all because there was a
bare possibility that some poor rag . . . or crumb of comfort might reach some
poor devil of a German somewhere. Your letter came on a later mail than the one
referred to in the clipping. So the U.S. Government is unable to send its mail on
the Canadian boats any more, either going or coming. "Britannia rules the waves,"
you know, and so she can waive the rules of common decency and respect for
other people's rights. We didn't happen to get any mail on the date referred to in
the enclosed article. Mrs. Janniske told me Sunday that her husband—who belongs*

*to the pilot association—took out a U.S. transport the day before which was to
carry the mail to San Francisco in order to keep it out of British hands. After that
first trouble, the U.S. Government ordered the Postal Agency here to use Japanese
mail boats, but I suppose that didn't prove safe either, as Japan is Britain's ally.
Nice, isn't it?*

. . . . Well, I must leave room for the pickle recipe

Sandwich pickles

¼ pint best olive oil

1 oz. celery seed

1 oz. white mustard seed

1 oz. black mustard seed

2 cups cider vinegar

*2 or more large onions, chopped fine. Wash and slice cucumbers to fill gallon
jar. Put in vinegar. Let stand three hours. Drain, and place in alternate layers
with the above dressing. Cover with cold vinegar. Let stand a few days. Can.*

Goodbye Love & best wishes
Tiam, Mae, Nelson and Alason

*enclose news article 9/19/16   American commercial /ass[n]. in China protest
censorship.*

November 9, 1916

Dearest Mother, Dad, and Gwen,—

*. . . . Miserably cold and windy weather we are having now. Tiam has two long
rides in it each day, but is wearing fur-lined underclothes this winter. They are a
better protection against the wind than the heaviest flannel. He sold the book to
the publishing company last week, so that he is thru with it now—except spending
the money. (Tho that is not an impossible task in Shanghai with war prices.) He
got a nice fat roll from the company, tho,—almost $200, and the value of the free
copies he is to receive will bring it to over $250. It is so much less trouble to sell it
outright than to retain the copyright ourselves.*

*You ask me how my Chinese is progressing, but I should rather say I could give
a more satisfactory account of the progress your Chinese son is making in the
Scotch dialect. You know he is teaching higher English Literature, and one of his
classes is studying Barrie's "Little Minister," which contains considerable dialect.
Anyway it taxes all my resources including Webster's Unabridged and supplement,
the glossary in my copy of Burn's Poems, all the recollections I can scrape up
of what I learned from you, to say nothing—or at any rate "the less said, the
better"—about the not-too-reliable—fabrications of my imagination. But anyhow,*

the result is that I have wakened in the middle of the night to hear a sentence in "Broad Scotch" wafted sleepily in my direction. By the way, here is a poem which you perhaps have laughed at already as it is from " Country Life." I got it from a British paper here, one of the very few worth while selections from the vast deluge of war poetry that has clogged the wheels of journalism for so long. . . .

"Weel," the "Little Minister" is a grand book, anyway, tho I don't believe you were "ower fond o't", much better morally than Hardy's "Return of the Native", which they had last year. The copy used is the "Maude Adam's" edition, with many photographic reproductions from the play as she gave it. Tiam is in love with Babbie already, tho we haven't even got to Nannie's tea party; but I am not jealous because, in fact, I am in love with her myself—(to say nothing of the little minister). Tiam has Macbeth in another class and Vicar of Wakefield in another. I tell him he is strong on Scotch and ministers this term. . . .

I dream time and time again that you have come here or I have gone there, and I talk myself hoarse every time. When I wake up it always seems as tho I had been with you. . . .

Good bye and good love and good luck!
FFF/Mae

Shanghai, China
Feb. 24, 1917

Dearest Mama, Dad and Gwen,—

. . . . Well, Mama, open your ears and your eyes to their widest extent to receive the most unthinkable of unthinkables: Here I sit in CHINA drinking Indian tea (from Lipton's in Calcutta). . . . I don't know what I said in that letter of December 15 that "set you to worrying about Tiam." It is impossible to make an unqualified statement to the effect that he is well, or even out of danger. But past experience has taught him to be careful, to recognize the danger signals and how to avoid the repeated injuries to his lungs. A month of continuous neglect and I tremble to think of the consequences. But yet he looks well and appears active. So infinitely better than dozens I see every day on the streets. His face is full and the color good, and so long as he can keep a good appetite and get plenty of rest, I feel that he is as safe as any one can be in these days of "battle, murder, and sudden death." Oh! when I think of the battle fields of Europe with their thousand unspeakable tortures, and the millions of lonely waiting women with the thots of those tortures ever present in their minds, it seems to me that the woman whose husband is beside her . . . enjoys the most priceless blessing in the power of Heaven to bestow. . . . You know, Mama, Tiam leaves here at ten o'clock in the morning and gets back at half-past three or half-past four. Then at five he goes to the Law School and gets back about eight. On the days when I teach, I leave here at one o'clock, and get back a little after five. So, on those days I don't see him from ten in the morning until eight at night, usually. But it happens that in going to the Law School he travels for about a mile over the road by which I come home, so by watching closely for that distance I sometimes catch a glimpse of him for a second in passing. I always watch; and when I do see him, I am as delightedly happy as—well, as tho it were years ago in Ann Arbor and I was just beginning to suspect that I loved him. Oh! I'm happier than that. Much as I miss you and would like to have us all together again, yet I am happier than I ever was before in my life. And I don't think you will be sorry to know that, or feel that I love you any the less. For, after all, marriage—if it is anything at all—is the biggest thing in the world.—And a man who can be trusted on the continent, can be trusted off it, too, or on any other continent,—tell Aunt Julia—It's just as I told that woman way back in Ann Arbor: "If a man isn't worth going anywhere in the world for, he isn't worth marrying in the first place." And with Tiam I would willing go to the North Pole, the South Pole, or the equator,—yes, even to the moon, "and I don't care how you spell it."

. . . . We had a big laugh over the fortune teller. Can't see the remotest chance of our coming to America in 1918. [The Frankings did return to the States in 1918.] But of course, you never can tell. It's something to dream over, at any rate. . . . Alason is growling a sleepy-song in the arms of his nurse, Little beggar. He likes me to "sing him to sleep" . . . and I made him a nice lullaby, too . . . to the tune of "I Wonder Who's Kissing Her Now. . . . I pieced together all the appropriate fragments I could think of.
"O sleep little baby of mine,"
for mother is holding thee close;
Her arms are about thee, her smile above
Slumber, then, soft repose. . . .
O sleep little baby of mine
the slumber by melody won
Thou art our own radiance from Heaven to shine,
Our bright golden "ray of the sun" . . .

Now love and best wishes as usual from
FFF/Mae

289 Ave. Joffre
Shanghai, China
June 26, 1917

Dear Mother and all,—

Well, my exam papers are all corrected, but I still have the marks for the term's work to fix up. And I shall probably help Tiam with his two hundred or more papers. I can't do the Law Exam. papers, but the English ones I can, of course, and it is some help, especially now when he is so busy. He has recently been appointed Legal Advisor for the Bureau of Foreign Affairs here in this province (Kulangsu). The Bureau is located here at Shanghai. The present commissioner is the new man this year, but Tiam knew him before he came here, and has been able to help him in various ways. There is some salary with position, but more honor than money, as the Commissioner is practically the leading Chinese in the city here. If it is necessary to bring any cases for the government, the fee for that is extra. Then Tiam is considering several propositions of getting back into active law work, as he feels his health is better than before and he is anxious to resume that as soon as possible. He has made no definite decision yet, however, whether to join some firm or start a new one.

As I said before, this is a difficult subject, especially to write about, but I do hope you will take this, at least, in the spirit in which I write. I think I have experienced enough to be sure of one thing: There is such a thing in the world as racial intermarriage; but, like the art of poetry, people must be born for it. Such people could be content with no other kind of union. But to those who are not born for it, the attempt would be a disastrous experiment. Then, out of the thousands of Chinese students in America, a small percent—I do not know how small, but say one in two thousand—has the firm desire of bringing home a foreign wife,—and the moral courage and strength of purpose necessary to such an undertaking. But even if another one out of five thousand should find his way to your friendship, you no longer have the other half of the combination to justify such encouragement. . . .

Love & kisses
Tiam, Mae, Nelson & Alason

289 Ave. Joffre
Shanghai, China
July 9, 1917

Dear Mother and all,—

. . . . We gave a dinner last week at the Astor House,—THE hotel in Shanghai. It's a beautiful one, too. Entertained the Commissioner for Foreign Affairs, the

Judge of the United States Supreme Court for China, and some others. (Oh, we have entertained Ex-ambassadors, railway and College Presidents, and all varieties of large-dimensioned ones, too. But what's the use of writing about it? In fact, it is so hard to choose the things you care to hear about).

(Say, Dad, the Judge is a native of Nebraska). . . .

Tiam is busy getting his new office opened. He is to be associated with another lawyer in the same building, so that he can hand over any work in case of necessity. It will be less hard on him, I think, than before. And he is also to undertake less school work.

Things have been pretty busy here, too, on account of the government situation, as Shanghai is a Republican stronghold, you know. There were hundreds of five-bar flags displayed on the 4th. The 4th was celebrated in grand style by the Americans and all the allies; and the Chinese decided to hang out their flag in honor of the day and also as political declaration of their own. The flag displays are always interesting here. For example, when any one of the allies has a national holiday, the tram cars are decorated accordingly: on the French tram-line each car carries at each end two French flags, with the flag of the nation celebrating in the middle. . . . The arrangement is the same with British flags, of course, instead of French. On days of general rejoicing the flags of all the principal allies are carried. Shanghai is an interesting place, for everybody who is not German. I don't know what Mrs. Bauer found to write about, but I often think that if she could live in a British community her miserable chickens of race prejudice would come fluttering home to roost, and she'd find out just what vile scum of the earth she belongs to. Not that I really think they are, of course, any more than Chinese are all the things she thinks they are. Please remain seated while the subject is being changed. The boy says Tiffin is served, only he says it in Chinese. . . .

Now I seem to be approaching the end of my paper, with just about room enough left to say good-bye. Hope for another letter soon. (You may consider that sentence declarative or imperative,—or both.)

Lovingly,
Mae

Amoy, China
December 18, 1917

[typewritten]
Dear Mother,—

I hope by the time the postman hands this in, you will already have received my last letter of December 2nd or thereabout, announcing the safe return of the Franking Family to China, together with the safe arrival in the world at large of the Fifth of the Family. And I hope that the sudden and unexpected acquisition of a new granddaughter didn't prove too much of a shock.

Well, she was three weeks old yesterday, this Chinese granddaughter of yours, and she hasn't been thrown to a single solitary lobster yet. In fact, I doubt if the lobsters could get her even by coming after—now. Of course, grandsons are highly desirable citizens; but there are three of them in the family already, (Tiam's brother now has a little boy about a year old), while SHE happens to be the first daughter in two generations on this side of the water, and that's some distinction. Moreover, her grandma in showing her off to the neighbors always tells them that she looks just as Tiam used to when he was little, especially her mouth and chin, which is what I discovered myself before we had left Swatow. And, any how, Mama, if you could only hold her yourself for five minutes I believe you would go back to your "old love", (girls, I mean).

Nelson has been perfectly delighted with her from the first minute he saw her; began planning right away that as soon as baby sister got big enough, he would take hold of one hand and Alason would take hold of the other and they'd run fast; also that when he was big enough he would take baby sister for an automobile ride: she would sit in the back seat and he would turn the steering wheel. For the first few days he spent most of the time within six inches of her nose—more or less. Alason has never been the least bit jealous of her tho he is sometimes jealous of Nelson. At the beginning he walked around with his hands behind his back, wearing a somewhat puzzled expression and the air of one reserving judgment. Now he wants to kiss her a dozen times whenever he comes near, and expects anyone else present to do the same, tho most of us don't wait for his invitation.

Nelson and Alason are both wearing Chinese winter clothes, and I have to look two—often three—times to avoid getting them mixed up with the neighbors' children. but then, Lou didn't consider the possibility of my having Chinese neighbors when she called attention to that advantage. . . .

Tiam mailed that last letter of mine on December 4th, and got yours of October 4th. Took it just two months to reach us, and it is postmarked Ann Arbor, Manila, Cebu, Amoy, and Kulangsu, besides having three Chinese stamps, the "censored" seal, and the forwarding directions on it,—altogether a most interesting letter, both inside and outside. . . .

I neglected to say in the last letter that the baby and I were "doing well", but I thot you would know that everything must be all right or we couldn't be up and off in a week. You see, I wasn't looking for any baby until about the Sixth of December; I even had a faint hope of holding that kind of a birthday party. At first we thot some of waiting in Cebu until after the baby was born, but medical arrangements there were not at all satisfactory; and it seemed much easier also to cross the China Sea with two children again than with three. Moreover, there is a good hospital here in Kulangsu, the foreign settlement, and we planned that Tiam would have the boys at home with his mother while I was in the hospital. But you ken what Bobbie Burns said. Tho if our steamer from Cebu to Hong Kong had not been delayed and delayed all along the way, there would still have been plenty of time. For I don't think she came a day too soon: she was perfect in every way. Just another argument in support of that theory in your green book: that young ladies come early to their appointments, and that if anybody is late of course, Mama, you might know it would be a young gentleman. Then, too, Swatow is famous for laces, embroideries, and jams, so I suppose, having an eye to the future, she decided that it was a most auspicious place for a girl to make a start in life. If I had any idea of her intentions when we were on shore in the morning, instead of about three hours before her arrival, we could have made all arrangements then, and have avoided much hurry and anxiety, which I found most upsetting, and which was the only difficulty I encountered myself. We had a Japanese doctor and midwife (who was also the doctor's wife), and the attendance was very satisfactory. She came every day to wash and dress the baby and fix me up, and we also had a Chinese amah. But Tiam certainly had a strenuous time for a man out in search of health. It is occasions like that which show what a person is made of,—if one doesn't know already—and if I had possessed a gold medal set with diamonds, I would have considered it too cheap to present to him. He is better and stronger of course, vastly better than when we left Shanghai, but I want to see still more improvement, and hope that our visit here will effect it. More about that next time. Just now I must close and get ready to go up to the city with Tiam. . . .

F.F.F./Mae

P.S. Forgot the most important part: Her name, it appears, is Cecile. "Cecile Franking".

Peking, China
March 12, 1918

Dearest,—

Well, I have been slow getting this letter to you. After I moved to the Y.M.C.A., I have made arrangement with Mr. Chu as to mails coming to his place, indicated above, tho I am still in the Y.M.C.A. After I wrote last, I attended a dinner given by Mr. Kang, the Vice-minister of the Agriculture. I met one Mr. Hwang, who was in the A.A. conference Oratorical contest. He is in the Ministry of Foreign Affairs. Mr. Chu took me to the theater the other night. I met a fellow who is going to be a consul in Rangoon, Burma. In fact I met many fellows who are all holding some positions. Many of them teaching in Gov't Peking Uni.

I met Dr. Kuo this evening, who is here at the request of the Minister of Education. I took him to dinner in a hotel where I met Frank Upham. I feel that I may have a chance some where if I wait long enough, especially I am trying to appear rich & independent & not in hurry to seize any job except a fat one. Anyway, that is the impression I created on Chu, Huwang, etc. The only way for me to get the desired post is to know the proper man in the Ministry. To be sent out as consul or mixed ct. magistrate I must know the ministers in the office of Foreign Affairs. To be sent out as a judge, I must know the ministers of the Board of Justice. However, the Mixed Ct. Magistrate in Kulangsu seems to me more probable, as soon as Mr. Sheu is out or promoted. He is not even a graduate, I understood now. At any rate, I shall try to stand the expenses here for at least six months & if necessary, I shall be willing to get hold of teaching position somewhere for next fall. But this is my chance to wait for an appointment of some sort, since I am here for this purpose. I may never have the chance again. Should I succeed—it means comfort & ease for us all in the years to come. Should I fail—I can try to get something which would give us enough to live. I feel I can find something if I am not particular. Well, only a little sacrifice on our part—we can not hope for some good thing without paying a little for it.

I like the place quite well—as it is very much like the dormitory for students in America. I am beginning to recall my student's days spirit of work & push. The city is ok. Should I have the chance to be here, I don't mind living in Peking. Of course, the people you see on the streets are poor & dirty & the Chinese homes are low generally, but the better class occupy such big buildings, especially the officials & the foreign residents. There will be a returned students conference on Mar 23 & 24, & I have registered to attend by paying $2—Once a while I have to be generous about spending the money & it seems a sort of necessity.

The bank note I brot from Amoy is only equal to $.50 in Peking I have about $130—now, but forced by circumstances I have to [use] my letter of credit—on $1—at $1.30 If you can make her understand that . . . Amoy bank note $1— exchange Peking money at half dollar or fifty cents. It maybe necessary that I shall have to ask her to send me some money. But wait till I write you again— I will tell you in my next letter, if necessary. I wrote her a Chinese letter intended to give different impression on outsider's mind. If she asked you about me—just tell her "Tiam Hock iah Le Lieng h'au Ki-hue" T.H. still waiting for opportunity.

Oh yes, I attended the Union Church service here Y.M.C.A. Sunday eve. It is the same as Sunday service in Shanghai. I met a few Foreign devils & that Petres of Shanghai. Rumors all over the country that fighting are going on everywhere— but I feel that you are safe in Kulangsu—a settlement far from danger—not the same as on the Amoy side. As to me, I feel safe now—it is for that reason that I moved here for better protection. There may be fighting in Peking again, but I don't think it would amount to any thing. . . . By the way, there are about a dozen or more Chinese married foreign wives. The present Minister of Foreign Affairs has an Eng. wife. . . . I read in the paper that a petition has been sent to the gov't— prohibiting Chinese students abroad to marry foreign wife. The secretary of Y.M.C.A. here asked me whether we are happy or not about our marriage. I said—I couldn't get a better & happier wife. Shut his mouth. Well, I shall come for you or send for you when the proper time comes. I don't feel that it is advisable to take you away so soon. Besides we want to establish a home by finding some substantial job first. This is really the best time for us to have this change. Twice my health is poor—it is a necessary rest for me, & we have 3 kids, that is enough. In fact, we beat most of people that are our contemporaries. Some not even marry yet others have only 1 kid. Some body told me that Dr. Juo has married a second wife. Tho he kept silent. He has 2 kids. Mr. Kee of Nanking died leaving a widow & 1 kid. That "fool" has 1 kid & took his wife to Manila, & some one told me that his wife is in love with a fellow whom she used to know in America. Don't know anything about the truth of this. She is niece of Dr. Kuo.

Well, this is a fat letter and a good deal of news.

With love,
Tiam   XX

F. 104 Lah Kee Tah,
Kulangsu, Amoy
China Mar. 20, 1918

[typewritten]
Dear Mother, Dad and Gwen,—

Your letter of February 4th came last Wednesday (March 13), and I certainly laughed over your description of how you received the news about the young lady who upset our plans at Swatow. I succeeded, then, in "breaking the news gently". Well, March 13th is a pretty late date to be getting an answer to a letter of December 4th. I thot you must be "awful mad", or else that the shock had proved fatal[.] I was positive I pencilled a P.S. to that first letter, giving our address here. Was that in the second one, then? And didn't I tell you that Tiam's mama sent me back to bed for another week, for the Chinese consider that it takes a month to restore the system to normal? And didn't I say that my pretty little sister-in-law stayed in bed for 33 or 34 days, and my Chinese mama thot there was some difference between that and getting up on the seventh day for a steamer trip? She is always comparing the two of us, it seems, and not exactly to the advantage of her Chinese daughter-in-law. Perhaps I oughtn't to mention that, but I thot you would like to hear it, in view of all the past.

We have very good times together, altho we cannot do much visiting, for I don't speak much Amoy yet. You see I have to unlearn practically all the Chinese I used at Shanghai, and learn another dialect. Lately I have been helping her make Chinese shoes for Alason and his little cousin, and it seems quite romantic, tho ordinarily one wouldn't suppose there was anything romantic about shoes. But I keep thinking how surprised we were, ten years ago, when Tiam said that in China the women made their own shoes at home; I didn't think then that some day I would be helping his mama to make some.

Today I made ice-cream for them in a cunning little freezer sent from the Philippines. Of course, Mama, you know how I made it, and they enjoyed it very much. There is an artificial ice factory here, for the natural article is almost unknown—altho they say that a little did form this year at a point near here, to the great astonishment of the natives.

It is terribly lonely without Tiam. I tell him his mother had just been able to really get acquainted with him for the first time since he left her to go to the Philippines, years and years ago, and so it is harder for her to lose him again. Steamers are so scarce and infrequent now. The one on last Saturday brot us three letters from him at Peking, and gave his definite address there. So I was able to send the one I had been writing—an installment each evening—since the day he left. His mama counted the pages and laughed and laughed—there were thirteen of them, this size and finely written. We heard from him while in Shanghai, of course, but on account of the infrequent mails I didn't risk sending him any letter there. He likes Peking very much; says it is "such a nice big Oriental city, with large buildings and wide streets". Well, Kulangsu just suits me; I have to be careful and not let myself become too much attached to it. I never experienced four consecutive months of such uniformly delightful weather in all my life before. You wished for a slice of Philippine weather in one of your letters; but "you know not what you ask". Of course, if you could dilute it with a Michigan winter it wouldn't be half bad; but we saw the best of it, as I explained at the time, and to me that was just barely bearable and no more. Tho if Tiam had decided to stay there, I should have managed to endure it somehow. (There are some mountain health resorts which are quite famous.) He could have stayed, of course; but the ones who are, altho they make money all right, feel sort of expatriated, and his father wanted him to have his work in China. (The climate of China is by no means unhealthful, you know. Shanghai has the reputation of being blessed with the worst one in the whole country, and I quite believe it true.) So I am glad that he could please me and his papa at the same time. He has such a nice papa—almost good *enough for his mama, I decided. His manner is very pleasing and not at all "bear-bitey", as I fancied he would be. He doesn't speak very much English, but he speaks (reads and writes) Spanish, and of course he also uses Amoy and Visaya, the Philippine dialect used in Cebu. Oh! if the years I wasted on Latin and German could only have been put on Chinese and Spanish, the time might have been spent to some purpose. Is Gwen studying Russian?*

Well, the Russian Jews are supposed to be very fine people. You told me a long time ago that he was one. Let me tell you, while we are in that part of Europe, (tho I have probably told you before, for I forget from one letter to the next what has been said and what not) that the Russians do know how to make dill pickles. I got some from a German market in Shanghai several times, and knew that I have never eaten dill pickles before (nor have I since) and that you, Dad, have never eaten them at all. They were flavored with dill, and they were sour like sauerkraut, not vinegar, and also some hot, and they were some pickles. . . .

Nelson has just begun his first term of school. But don't expect a letter in six weeks. You wouldn't be able to read it, even if he should be able to write it, which he won't. For he is a Chinese boy going to a Chinese school,—the school of the Reformed Church mission here, which is only three doors away from us, so that we can see them playing in the yard from our upper front porch here. They teach in the local dialect, which he hasn't learned extremely well yet; but I think the discipline will be good for him, even tho he may not learn so much this first term. There is a fine kindergarten here, but too far away for him. Tiam has a cousin here, about thirteen years old, who is also attending this same school. . . .

Now Mama Dee, I must stop, for it is getting late. I hope you all are keeping well, and happy in spite of the war. Do you think it has made any great change in the people as a whole?

> *Love and best wishes from us all,*
> *and so Goodbye,*
> *Mae*

Consulate-General of the Republic of China
617 Montgomery Street
San Francisco, CAL. U.S.A.
December 15, 1918

Dear Mother, Dad & Gwen,—

You are hereby officially informed that Miss Cecile Franking, under the direct personal escort of two parents and a like number of brothers, arrived in San Francisco, California, U.S.A. on Friday, December 13 on the T.K.K. S.S. "Siberia Maru" from Amoy, China, via Hong Kong, Shanghai, Nagasaki, Kobe, Yokohama, and Honolulu. And when you've said that, you've said it all.

Awfully glad to find your two letters of Nov. 29, & Dec. 6 also Gwen's of Dec. 3, waiting for us at the consulate. We wrote you from Yokohama, and hope it was mailed in time to come on the "Siberia" with us, for then you will have it by now. So long since we had heard from you, I was almost afraid to open the letters, and so very thankful to find that you all lived and did well, same as we'uns. Say Mom! "Ain't it funny, tho?" When I was on my way from the continent the shot was fired that precipitated the war; and now when I started out to return to it (the continent) I no sooner reach Hong Kong than the war is over. (Makes me feel as big as the wind when he blew out the moon.)

We are all well, as I intimated above. The sea voyage was just what Alason needed, apparently, as he is ever so fat and happy looking now. Cecile also gained, but Nelson lost a pound or two, tho he is feeling all right in every way.

This is only a short note to let you know of our safe and sane arrival. We are stopping temporarily at the Argonaut Hotel, but looking for some permanent location; so you can continue to send our mail to the Consulate-General (Better address it to Tiam, tho instead of me). Will write often as I can, and tell you more about us, and try to answer some of your many questions. Hope you will reciprocate as usual, tho you have done more than your share of the writing all these years.

> *Bushels of love and kisses from us all.*
> *F.F.F./Mae (Mother, here's your girl).*

> *617 Montgomery Street*
> *San Francisco, CAL. U.S.A.*
> *Feb. 2, 1918 [should be 1919]*

Dear Mother, Dad & Gwen,—

I started you a letter Jan 29, but only wrote about three-fourths of a page, and haven't been able to finish it since, so will make a new beginning, altho it is almost 12 o'clock (at night).

Tiam has been sick in bed for over two weeks now. I think he did too much while I was sick, for he kept getting weaker all the time until finally he had to give up & go to bed. This last week we have had the doctor coming every day until today. He treated him for his stomach, on the theory that when the food eaten is properly digested & assimilated the supply of red blood produced will build up the lungs & stop the cough. Sounds reasonable to me, because I have been telling him ever since we got to S. Frisco that he'd never be able to eat enough to cure his trouble until his stomach had been fixed up. . . . Now he is going to try and get up

*again to get back to work, but he is still dreadfully weak, altho he has been up &
around the rooms more or less during the whole time. I feel very worried
sometimes, and then sometimes I am hopeful again.*

*Mama, your nice newsy letter of Jan 17, was received some few days ago &
much appreciated, the pencil in no wise detracting from our enjoyment of it. We
are very happy over the prospect of a visit from dear old Dad this coming summer.
Have been wanting to ask you all, to come, but was afraid you'd think that just the
sight of us wouldn't justify spending so much of your hard-earn savings. We've got
plenty of room, and by summer everything will be all "evened off." I looked up the
return fare . . . even before we left China, and it's somewhere about $110, and you
might get excursions rates later in the season—July or August, won't it be a great
trip tho? Think of it, Dad!—out across the "rolling prairies" (do they roll same as
they did thirty-odd years ago?) and then farther across the mountains, & finally to
arrive here in little old 'Frisco—three grand children to play with and you with
not a whisker to be pulled! Nelson wants to know whether Dad will come on the
train or boat, and is planning all sorts of things to build with his construction
blocks for Dad's entertainment. It will be a great event for him to renew acquaintances
with Dad. . . . Alason is getting to be a perfect dickens for mischief of all sorts.
He's as broad as he's tall; his cheeks are red & his eyes the blackest in the family.
His hair (which fell out considerably during his sickness) is coming in much darker.
Cecile is comical as a circus clown, when she isn't as sweet as a meadow violet "born
to blush unseen." Her chief occupation just now is irritating Nelson. Yesterday they
were looking at magazines, and Nelson held up his to point to a picture. "Mama!,"
he said, "What's this horse looking at?" And immediately Cecile called "Mama!"
and when she was sure of my undivided attention she ran her little finger over a
picture in her book & gravely inquired "Boo chick a boo boo?" Doesn't seem to
be in any hurry about talking real words, I mean, tho she adds new ones to her
[vocabulary] gradually. Then, yesterday they were playing with Tiam's traveling
bag, & Nelson, picked it up, said, "See Mama! I can hold it up with one hand."
The minute he set it down, Cecile grabbed my chair with her left hand and the bag
with her right, and straightening away up, "big" as Nelson & we properly appreciated
her achievement. She's very strong, anyway. Oh, they are all lots of comfort &
amusement, along with the care & responsibility. It's such fun to watch them play
together. When Nelson & Alason get into an altercation and have to be scolded,
Cecile helps me—too funny for anything. I can discipline the boys easily enough,—
too easily perhaps. But when it comes to Cecile—that is another matter. Whether
because she is a girl, & our only one, or because I am blessed with Dad's propensity
for showing every indulgence on the youngest & "taking it out" of the older ones. I
don't know yet. But if I so much as slap her fingers—persistently, defiantly naughty*

little fingers as they know how to be!—Oh! she puts such a note of heartbreak into her cry; she bends herself forward & bows her little head in such an utter abandonment of grief & despair—a tragic picture of hopeless, helpless, friendless woe—that I just naturally have to squeeze her up tight & kiss her more'n a million times, to let her know that her own little world is right side up after all.

Well, Mama Dee, still another day has gone by & my letter's not yet finished. But day times I am too busy, and evening too tired or discouraged to write a decent letter. There are so many things I want to tell you of the children, ourselves, & our surroundings. But it takes time & thot. And meanwhile you are waiting in vain for a letter. February 8. Well, I will close this letter up, as I am just going out to buy some things, and perhaps you will get it for a valentine. Tiam isn't up yet, tho he is better in some ways.

Love and best wishes from all,
Mae

725 California St.
San Francisco, Calif.
Feb. 19, 1919

Dear Mother and all,—

It has been over a week since I wrote to you last, and I hope you have not been worried. In spite of much help with the work from our neighbors here, I have had very little opportunity to write letters. The day after my last one was written, we decided to have the doctor for Tiam,—Mrs. William's doctor, that is. He is still on the case, and Tiam has a great deal of confidence in him. Thinks he is younger, more energetic & more thoro than the former M.D. He makes a very careful examination & study of Tiam's condition & he decided that it was Bronchia-pneumonia, following a mild attack of the "Flu". Also discovered the tubercular "bugs" in the "specimens" he took for the laboratory, but he can't say how far that trouble has progressed until this temporary condition clears up.

Tiam is able to sit up pretty well, but he can't walk without help. I guess he has never been so sick before. . . . Poor Boy! You would feel sad to see how thin & weak he is. But the hardest part seems to be over, and we all feel that he is getting better now. It must necessarily be slow & tedious work, however.

The rest of us are getting along all right. The children are well & fat, & Cecile is beginning to run alone pretty well these days. So many little things I'd like to say, but I can't stop for a longer letter now. I hope this will relieve any anxiety you may have felt, & I will write that personal & possessive also objective letter to you, Mama Dee, soon as I have the opportunity.

Mrs. W. is a great deal of help to us, & as she is alone in a two room *apartment, it is company for her, too. So I don't worry. But I am pretty busy just the same, with the three babies.*

Now I must close, and hope to get it out to you tomorrow. It is now getting on toward twelve o'clock & I must be getting on toward bed. Love & best wishes from us all, & remember Dad! We're looking forward to next summer.

FFF/Mae

Ku-Lang-Su
by
Mae Franking

We build our Eden—my love and I—
On an isle in the China Sea,
Where the rough gray rocks are hidden by
A tangle of vine and tree;
Where like rosy lanterns aglow at even
The ripe pomegranates sway,
And the tips of our tiled roofs point toward Heaven
In the quaint old Chinese way.

Chorus

Let us leave the west with its great unrest,
Beloved, let us toil no more!
These ships that wait at the Golden Gate
all sail for that far home-shore
   Where on the breast
   Of the China Sea
   Our Isle of the Blest
   Waits for you and me.
   Take me home with you
   To Ku-lang-su
We'll return to our Eden—my love and I—
When the great gold Chinese moon
Smiles down from a dusky purple sky
Where the soft night breezes croon
Through our Chinese courtyard of bamboo and willow
And the clustering dragon's eyes;
and we shall forget our every sorrow
In this new-old paradise.

[*Hand-written version of the above with this extra stanza*]

There's a fair little, rare little island
On the breast of the China Sea.

Its rugged outlines softened
By a tangle of vine & tree
Where pomegranates sway like lanterns—
Small globes of rosy light
And dragon's eyes hang in clusters
Of fruity-sweet delight.
There on a sunny hill slope
Is a home with its walls of gray
The tips of its tiled roof point toward Heaven
In the quaint old Chinese way.
And in the Chinese courtyard
Where fragile orchids bloom
The very flagsteps wait, I know,
For my love & me to come.

NOTES

Foreword

1. Katherine Anne Porter to Donald Stalling, 28 March 1956, Katherine Anne Porter Collection, McKeldin Library, University of Maryland.

2. Katherine Anne Porter, *The Collected Essays and Occasional Writings of Katherine Anne Porter* (New York: Delacorte Press, 1970), 91.

3. Edward Schwartz, "Katherine Anne Porter: A Critical Biography," Introduction by Robert Penn Warren, *Bulletin of the New York Public Library* 57 (May 1953): 211–247.

4. Porter's inscription in the McKeldin Library's copy of *My Chinese Marriage* is dated 2 June 1969.

5. Porter used the same reference in her 1941 introduction to Eudora Welty's *A Curtain of Green*.

6. Katherine Anne Porter, *The Collected Short Stories of Katherine Anne Porter* (New York: Harcourt, Brace and World, 1965), vi.

7. Katherine Anne Porter to Josephine Herbst, 18 March 1929, Beinecke Library, Yale University.

8. Porter, *Collected Essays*, 489.

9. Porter, *Collected Stories*, 326.

10. Collection of Joan Givner.

11. Katherine Anne Porter to Genevieve Taggard, 14 November 1924, McKeldin Library, University of Maryland.

12. Virginia Woolf, *A Room of One's Own* (London: Hogarth Press, 1929), 114.

13. Eudora Welty, "My Introduction to Katherine Anne Porter," *Georgia Review,* 44 1/2 (Spring/Summer 1990): 13–27.

14. *Katherine Anne Porter Conversations,* ed. Joan Givner (Jackson: University Press of Mississippi, 1987), 80.

Introduction

1. M. T. Franking, *My Chinese Marriage* (New York: Duffield, 1921); hereafter referred to as *MCM.* The Duffield edition is the one used for this text; a few typographical errors have been corrected.

2. *Asia* had published an early Porter story titled "Adventures of Hadji" (*Asia* 20 [August 1920]: 683–684). "A tale of a Turkish coffee-house, retold by Katherine Anne Porter." See Edward Schwartz's Porter bibliography.

3. Katherine Anne Porter's letter to Babette Deutsch, in the latter woman's papers at the New York Public Library. The letter was written while she stayed at the Hotel Allenel in Ann Arbor, Michigan, and is presumed to be dated after 4 September 1920.

4. Joan Givner, *Katherine Anne Porter* (New York: Simon and Schuster, 1982), 149. See letter Katherine Anne Porter wrote to Donald Stalling, 28 March 1956, Katherine Anne Porter Collection, McKeldin Library, University of Maryland.

5. John Foord, ed., "Contributors and Contributions," *Asia: The American Magazine on the Orient* 21 (August 1921): 657.

6. *Bulletin of the New York Public Library* 57 (May 1953). The quotation is from a letter Porter wrote on 7 November 1951 to the compiler of her bibliography by Edward Schwartz.

7. Katherine Anne Porter, ed., *What Price Marriage,* with Introduction and Notes (New York: J. H. Sears, ca. 1927). "Compiled with an introduction (signed 'Hamblen Sears') and notes by Miss Porter." See Edward Schwartz's Porter bibliography.

8. Edward Schwartz, *Katherine Anne Porter: A Critical Bibliography*. Folcroft, Penn.: Folcroft, 1953.

9. See Louise Waldrip and Shirley Ann Bauer, *A Bibliography of the Works of Katherine Anne Porter and a Bibliography of the Criticism of the Works of Katherine Anne Porter* (Metuchen, N.J.: Scarecrow Press, 1969).

10. Porter also said that this work did not belong on her list.

11. Joan Givner, *Katherine Anne Porter* (New York: Simon and Schuster, 1982), 150.

12. Holly Franking, "The Papers of Mae and Tiam Franking," Personal Collection. The dates of subsequent letters are cited in the text.

13. See selected letters of Mae in the Appendix.

14. *MCM* refers to Mae and Tiam as Margaret and Chan-King Liang, respectively. It also says that the two met while in college.

15. The college that Margaret and Chan-King Liang attend is not named in *MCM*, but it was the University of Michigan in Ann Arbor.

16. Tiam's father had an import/export business in Cebu in the Philippines.

17. *MCM* says Chan-King (Tiam) transferred to a New England university.

18. See Appendix for examples of Tiam's early love letters.

19. *MCM* does not mention this conflict.

20. See Appendix. The letters of this period show what a difficult time it was for both Tiam and Mae.

21. *MCM* does not mention this situation.

22. *MCM* drastically down-played the scandal the marriage caused in Ann Arbor, Detroit, Grand Rapids, and at the University of Michigan.

23. *MCM* gives a much fuller account of the family's life in China than do the letters.

24. See Appendix for the full text of some letters that Mae wrote to her parents from China between 1914 and 1918.

25. *MCM* gives a more complete account of the family's stay at the ancestral home in Amoy than do the letters. Amoy is now Hsia-men, situated in the southern hills of China, across the bay from Hong Kong.

26. Cecile M. Franking, "An Act of Solace," *New Yorker* 29 (1954): 24–25.

1. In America

1. Pseudonym for Tiam Hock Franking.

2. The college referred to is the University of Michigan in Ann Arbor. Actually, Mae and Tiam first met at Ann Arbor High School.

3. Ann Arbor, Michigan.

4. Mrs. Henry O'Dell Watkins, nee Munro.

5. Pseudonym for Mae Munro Watkins.

6. Amoy, China, now Hsia-men.

7. Cebu in the Philippines. Tiam's father, Basilio Ng Bun Dan, Esq., had an import and export business there.

8. See Appendix for letter Mae wrote to herself on 29 August 1909.

9. Tiam transferred from Ann Arbor High School to Central High School in Grand Rapids, Michigan. This move was made at the request of Mae's parents, who felt that Mae and Tiam needed some time apart to determine their true feelings for each other.

10. See Appendix for letter dated 22 April 1910.

11. Tiam attended the University of Michigan Law School. See Appendix for letter of 27 July 1910. Mae enrolled at the University of Michigan Department of Literature, Science, and the Arts on 21 August 1911.

12. Before Tiam and Mae decided to marry, Mae's relatives urged her to break relations with Tiam because of his nationality. See Appendix for excerpt of letter dated 26 October 1910 that Mae wrote to an aunt in defense of her relationship with Tiam.

13. Tiam's family also objected to the marriage, and Tiam was disinherited by his father when the marriage took place on 12 September 1912.

14. Tiam and Mae had a rather stormy courtship because of cultural and moral differences. Tiam thought that sex followed love; Mae thought sex followed marriage. See Appendix for letters of 1911.

15. After Tiam was disinherited, he worked as a waiter in Chinese restaurants to cover his expenses. He was also attending the Detroit College of Law.

16. The private ceremony got public notices on the front pages of the Ann Arbor, Detroit, and Grand Rapids newspapers. See the newspaper stories in the Appendix. The scandal of the interracial marriage forced Tiam and Mae to withdraw from the University of Michigan. See editorial in appendix objecting to such marriages. Tiam and Mr. and Mrs. Watkins were interviewed by the press. Tiam transferred to the Detroit College of Law, while Mae stayed at home to prepare for the baby. See Tiam H. Franking's letter to the editor of the *Ann Arbor Times*, 15 September 1912.

17. Tiam and Mae married on 12 September 1912 at the Watkins' home in Ann Arbor, Michigan. See Appendix for letters of 1912.

18. Tiam moved to Detroit, where he finished his law degree at the Detroit College of Law on 19 June 1913. See letter of same date. While there, he also became president of the Detroit Club of the Chinese Students' Alliance U.S.A. and continued his oratorical work. Tiam supported himself and his family by working as a waiter at the Oriental Cafe in Detroit.

19. This was 1912.

20. See photograph of Tiam with his parents.

21. The first child born to Tiam and Mae Franking was Nelson W. Franking. See

Appendix for Mrs. Watkins' letter of 6 January 1913, announcing the baby's birth to Tiam.

22. Pseudonym for Nelson W. Franking. The *W* is probably for Watkins, Mae's maiden name.

23. See Appendix for letters from 25 June 1913 through 1 January 1914 that describe Tiam's journey from Michigan to San Francisco and across the Pacific to Shanghai.

24. See Appendix for Mae's letter to Tiam dated 16 December 1913. Also see photograph of Tiam, Mae, and Nelson that was printed in the *Chung Sai Yat Po,* the Chinese daily paper of San Francisco, on 13 December 1913.

25. See Appendix for Tiam's letter from Shanghai dated 5 February 1915.

26. See Appendix for Mae's letter dated 21 January 1915.

27. See Appendix for Mae's letter of 5 July 1914, where she describes her trip to China.

28. Mae radically changed Tiam's plans for her because the Japanese steamer *Tenyo Maru* would not sail until August. See Appendix for Mae's explanation to Tiam in her letters of 28 April and 3 May 1914.

2. In Shanghai

1. See Appendix for Mae's letter dated 2 September 1915.

2. See Appendix for Mae's letters dated 12 and 22 February 1914 and 9 November 1916.

3. See Mae's letter dated 3 May 1915.

4. See Appendix for letters dated 3 May 1915, 2 September 1915, and 24 February 1917.

5. See Mae's letter dated 2 September 1915.

6. See Appendix for Mae's letter dated 19 September 1916.

3. First Daughter-in-Law

1. See Appendix for Mae's letters dated 25 July and 19 September 1916.

2. Alfred is a pseudonym for Alason Franking. See Appendix for Mae's letter dated 20 December 1915.

3. See Appendix for Mae's letters dated 15 and 21 January and 3 May 1915, and 26 June 1917.

4. Alicia is the pseudonym for Cecile Mae Franking. See Appendix for Mae's letters dated 18 December 1917 and 20 March 1918.

5. See Appendix for Mae's letter dated 12 March 1918.

4. The Eternal Hills

1. See photograph of the Watkins family.

2. See Appendix for Mae's letter dated 15 December 1918.

3. See Appendix for Mae's letters of 1919 and her poem "Kulangsu."

WORKS CITED

F., M. T. "My Chinese Marriage." *Asia: The American Magazine on the Orient* 21 (June 1921): 487–492, 546, 548, 550.

———. "My Chinese Marriage." *Asia: The American Magazine on the Orient* 21 (July 1921): 612–618, 648, 650.

———. "My Chinese Marriage." *Asia: The American Magazine on the Orient* 21 (August 1921): 715–720, 737–739.

———. "My Chinese Marriage." *Asia: The American Magazine on the Orient* 21 (September 1921): 781–787, 814.

Franking, Holly. "The Papers of Mae and Tiam Franking." Personal Collection.

Franking, M. T. *My Chinese Marriage.* New York: Duffield, 1921.

Givner, Joan. *Katherine Anne Porter.* New York: Simon and Schuster, 1982.

Schwartz, Edward. *Katherine Anne Porter: A Critical Bibliography.* Folcroft, Penn.: Folcroft, 1953.